1963/64 promotion-winning captain Charlie Hurley leads out stalwart full-backs Len Ashurst and Cec Irwin after Sunderland had returned to the top flight.

Also available at all good book stores

9781785316470

9781785313929

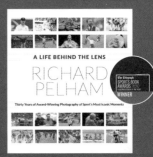

9781785315466

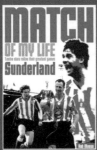

9781908051738

9781848182042

9781908051615

9781785317590

9781785317583

9781785317613

PROMOTION-WINNING
BLACK CATS

PROMOTION-WINNING
BLACK CATS

THE STORIES BEHIND
EACH AND EVERY SUNDERLAND AFC
PROMOTION SEASON

ROB MASON

First published by Pitch Publishing, 2021

Pitch Publishing
A2 Yeoman Gate
Yeoman Way
Worthing
Sussex
BN13 3QZ
www.pitchpublishing.co.uk
info@pitchpublishing.co.uk

ISBN 978 1 78531 793 4

Typesetting and origination by Pitch Publishing
Printed and bound in India by Replika Press Pvt. Ltd.

CONTENTS

Rob Mason is Sunderland AFC's official historian. He has watched the team since 1967, written for the programme since 1986 and spent almost two decades working full-time at the Stadium of Light editing the club's publications. During this time Sunderland won more Programme of the Year awards than any other club. He has written over 50 football books, including over 40 on Sunderland.

ACKNOWLEDGEMENTS

AS ALWAYS with any book there are many people to thank. Just like a goalscorer takes the headlines when the whole team have contributed, the author gets his or her name on the cover but can't achieve what they want to without a lot of assistance.

In my case the first people I want to thank are the players who so readily gave up their time to talk at length about the promotion campaigns they starred in. Every one of the people featured in *Promotion-Winning Black Cats* is extremely proud to have played for a club of Sunderland's stature and to be part of a success story. So often my interviews became even longer than planned, because after I'd finished my questions the tables would be turned as ex-players wanted to quiz me about the state of the club today. That showed me I'd made good choices in who I'd contacted. These are players with the club at heart and, of course, they are not the only ones as so many of their team-mates are just as committed. So my sincere thanks go to: Brian Usher, Dick Malone, Shaun Elliott, Paul 'Jack' Lemon, Tony Norman, Craig Russell, Allan 'Magic' Johnston, Stephen 'Sleeves' Elliott and (for Brazil he should play) Danny Collins. Additionally, my thanks go to Gordon Armstrong for contributing the foreword. Gordon appeared in the promotion seasons of 1987/88, 1989/90 and 1995/96, making more appearances in promotion seasons than anyone else.

I also must place on record my deep thanks to Andrew Smithson. The author of Dickie Ord's biography, Andrew was one of my A-team of contributors in the many years I edited the club's publications and is an extremely devoted Sunderland supporter. While I have made every effort to ensure this book is error-free I am massively indebted to Andrew. He took on the task of checking everything for me and thanks to his detailed feedback I realised that as well as making silly typos I had slipped up too many times. Any errors that remain are entirely mine alone but thanks to Andrew's attention to detail there are far fewer than if I didn't have such a tremendous colleague. As always with all the Sunderland books I write I also have to thank Mike Gibson, Barry Jackson and Niall McSweeney, who are always ready to check things out or clarify things for me, often matters of the most obscure nature and the sort of things the internet has still to find a way of retrieving!

Paul and Jane Camillin at Pitch Publishing do such a good job of bringing so many excellent books to readers and I hope this one maintains the standards they have set. I also have to thank Duncan Olner for producing the book cover.

Inspiration for this book came from Peter Rogers, a good friend and for many years my counterpart as programme editor at Norwich City. A walking encyclopaedia on the Carrow Road club, Peter sent me his 2019 book *Promotion-Winning Canaries* done with Pitch. The strong relationship between Sunderland and Norwich stems from the 1985 League Cup 'Friendly' Final and this volume sprang from his excellent book on his own club's promotions.

My better half Barbara has once again had to listen to me babbling on about SAFC and put up with me disappearing to go to matches or burn the midnight oil writing. Even though I do have a thesaurus she is also used to me interrupting what she is doing by shouting, 'What's another word for such and such?' when I realise I've repeated a couple of words close together!

Finally, thank you for buying this book because rather like teams have found when playing behind closed doors during the Covid-19 pandemic, just as playing football without fans is not the same, there is no point writing books if people aren't going to read them. I hope giving up your time to read what follows will bring back memories, provide a few smiles and ideally tell you some things you might not have known.

FOREWORD

FROM BEING a boy growing up surrounded by Newcastle United supporters on Tyneside, Sunderland were always my club, so I was thrilled to play for Sunderland in every one of my 416 appearances. Of these, 87 were league or play-off games in promotion seasons, which I've learned from this book means I played more games in promotion-winning campaigns than anyone else. All but one of these matches came as Denis Smith took us from the Third Division to the First in the space of three seasons from 1987/88 to 1989/90, and I was still around to appear in the opening game of the next promotion year in 1995/96.

I had some great times at Sunderland playing alongside some great players and characters, some of whom remain lifelong friends. Rob Mason has spoken to players from every one of the Lads' promotion-winning teams right back to the first from 1963/64. The stories of the promotion successes bring back a lot of memories and if you are too young to have enjoyed all of these seasons, then reading about the earlier ones will give you an insight into a series of successes.

To win promotion takes a whole season of effort. Players and staff always want to test themselves at the highest level possible, so a promotion success raises the bar as your prize is to earn the right to pit your wits against opponents from a higher division. For Sunderland to go from the third tier to the first in such a short space of time was an amazing journey and, of course, there were some great games along the way, not least the play-off semi-final against Newcastle in 1990.

Every one of the promotions carries its own excitement, its great goals and a squad of players who made it happen. Whether it is a player who took part in every game or someone who came in to play a handful of matches, they are part of the story. In this book of promotion wins, in addition to the memories of the seasons, every single player who played in a league game is profiled.

As we look to get this great club of ours back to where I feel it belongs at the top level, with our superb stadium, fantastic fan base and great history, I'm sure you will enjoy reading the red and white recollections of seasons we all enjoyed – even if at times they were nail-biting and had you scouring the league tables and remaining fixtures of promotion rivals for more hours than you care to admit!

Gordon Armstrong

Gordon Armstrong played in all 49 league and play-off games as promotion was won in 1989/90. He started 36 league fixtures and played in another as a sub in the 1987/88 promotion campaign. He also came off the bench to play in the opening match of the 1995/96 season when Sunderland went on to win the Championship. He is seventh in the all-time list of appearances in the entire history of the club.

INTRODUCTION

WHEN I was born promotion was a word Sunderland supporters didn't need to consider as the Lads had never been relegated. Until a couple of months after I came into the world as the son of two Roker Park regulars, Sunderland were the only club in the country who had only ever played in the top flight, a record they had held since before World War Two. Unfortunately, in my lifetime promotions have come along regularly because, sadly, there have been a lot of relegations as well.

I was six when Charlie Hurley captained the club to its first-ever promotion in 1964. I didn't start going until February 1967 although over the years I have been privileged to meet all of the regular XI from that first promotion season, many of them becoming personal friends. Sadly, several of that side have passed away in recent times but over the years, often at meetings of the excellent Sunderland Former Players' Association, the players of the deeply loved 1964 team have shown themselves to be absolute gentlemen as well as great players. Usually at such events I'm lost in football chat with various players and my long-suffering wife Barbara gets unintentionally left by me but, like the wives and widows of their team-mates, she will never be left to sit on her own as the Lads will bring her into conversation and ensure her glass is never empty. Indeed, whenever we have a bottle of Primitivo we toast the great, late Nicky Sharkey, who introduced us to his favourite red!

I saw most of the team of '64 in subsequent seasons and Monty was still there to play in the second promotion team of 1975/76. I was there in 1970 as defeat to Liverpool resulted in the second-ever relegation, and I've seen every promotion and relegation season since, often attending every match, home and away.

Brian Usher debuted on the opening day of the 1963/64 season and played in every game bar one. He talks us through that promotion season, while for the second in 1975/76 I spoke to Dick Malone, a member of the FA Cup-winning team of 1973 and someone who after missing the first two games of his promotion campaign went on to miss just one more in the season Sunderland won their second trophy under Bob Stokoe.

For the 1979/80 promotion winners my go-to man was Shaun Elliott, capped by England B at Roker Park during the season. Like Brian Usher he missed just one game in his promotion campaign. While that promotion took the Lads back into the top flight, by the time the next promotion came along Sunderland were looking to escape from a first-ever slide into the third tier. Paul 'Jack' Lemon played in 41 of the 46 league games. Two years later Lemon was squeezed out, being an unused sub on two occasions as Sunderland went up again.

That 1989/90 season saw the strangest of promotions. Sunderland defeated Newcastle United in the play-offs to reach Wembley where they lost to Swindon but still went up. Punished for being found guilty of a range of financial misdemeanours, Swindon were denied a promotion which Sunderland were awarded despite counterclaims from Newcastle, who had finished third in the table, and Sheffield Wednesday, who had been third from bottom in the top flight. Had Sunderland lost the play-off final heavily it could have been a much more difficult decision for the game's authorities to promote the Black Cats. Thankfully, keeper Tony Norman had a blinder at Wembley where he was only conquered by a deflection, so who better to talk us through those play-offs and the promotion campaign than Wales international Tony.

For the fifth promotion I turned from a stopper to a scorer and spoke to Craig Russell, top scorer in that celebrated 1995/96 season. Unlucky to be relegated a year later despite accruing 40 points, the following year Sunderland earned 90 points but still didn't go up, dramatically losing the play-off final on penalties to Charlton after a thrilling 4-4 draw. Coming back from that disappointment, Peter Reid's side achieved a record 105 points in a magical 1998/99. Left-winger Allan 'Magic' Johnston was fabulous that term but was then the subject of the gaffer's decision not to unleash him on the Premier League as Johnston entered the final year of his contract. Now a manager himself, 'Magic' discusses that sensational season and explains what happened as he didn't get the chance to return to the Premier League where he had scored Sunderland's last league goal at Roker Park in the club's previous top-flight campaign.

Striker Stephen 'Sleeves' Elliott and defender Danny Collins both played in the promotions of 2004/05 and 2006/07. They talk us through those contrasting campaigns under Mick McCarthy and Roy Keane, with Sleeves focussing on 2004/05, when he scored 15 league goals, and Collins concentrating on 2006/07, when only skipper Dean Whitehead started more games than Danny's 36.

Sunderland supporters have experienced too many of the lowest lows in football. Relegations with record low points tallies in 2003 and 2006 and eight successive Wembley defeats – including three on penalties – between 1985 and 2019. Those lows have a silver lining though. The lower the lows the higher the highs. If you support a team to whom finishing beneath the Champions League places is considered a disaster you have no idea of the levels of emotion Sunderland supporters have been through in recent decades. There are no more passionate supporters than the red and white army. *Promotion-Winning Black Cats* relives the times that make all the heartache worthwhile. I hope you enjoy reading the book as much as I've enjoyed talking to the promotion heroes and producing this latest addition to the recording of red and white history.

Sunderland need a tenth and 11th promotion to get back to the Premier League. It will be easier said than done but there is only one place for Sunderland to be and that is the top flight. Here's to the next chapters.

Rob Mason

1963/64 DIVISION TWO RUNNERS-UP

Winger Brian Usher debuted on the opening day of the season and went on to miss just one game as Sunderland won promotion and reached the FA Cup quarter-final.

MONTGOMERY, IRWIN, Ashurst, Harvey, Hurley, McNab, Usher, Herd, Sharkey, Crossan and Mulhall. The names of Sunderland's first-ever promotion team roll off the tongues of Sunderland supporters old enough to have seen them more easily than any of the club's other promotion sides. This is partly because they were such a settled XI in the days before substitutes and partly because they remain to this day a team deeply loved by the people who watched them.

Sunderland's first promotion didn't arrive until 1964 because, having become the first club to join the Football League's founder members in 1890, they had been the last club to lose the proud boast of only ever having played at the top level. That first relegation came in 1958. After two seasons struggling in the lower reaches they finished sixth in 1961 and had consecutive third-placed finishes before returning to what was considered their rightful place with promotion in 1963/64.

1962 had seen the Wearsiders miss out by a point after being held at lowly Swansea Town on the final day. A year later there was an even closer call. Top of the table with a game to go, just one point was needed from a home match with promotion rivals Chelsea, only for the Londoners to win with the scrappiest of goals. They went on to pip Sunderland to promotion on goal average after winning their outstanding game in hand 7-0 against Portsmouth.

Brian Clough had scored 24 goals in 24 games by Boxing Day 1962, when he suffered what was ultimately a career-ending injury. Later renowned as one of the game's most successful and charismatic managers, Cloughie had scored 63 times in 74 games for Sunderland. His place was taken by up-and-coming youngster Nick Sharkey, who soon became the only post-war player to score five times in a game for Sunderland, but inevitably he couldn't replace Clough's goals to games ratio and ultimately the Black Cats missed promotion by a whisker.

Having gone so close to promotion two years running in the days when only two teams went up and there were no play-offs, Sunderland and their fans were desperate to win a first-ever promotion. The opening fixture of 1963/64 took Sunderland to Huddersfield Town, a team who would have been in the play-offs the previous term had they existed. No easy start then, but goals in each half from Andy Kerr and George Mulhall got the campaign off to a fine start with a 2-0 victory.

Making his debut at Huddersfield was teenage winger Brian Usher. He would do so well he would miss just one of the 49 league and cup games. 'I remember Ray Wilson was left-back,' says Brian of his debut as a right-winger up against the man who would become a World Cup winner with England three years later. 'I got called into the practice games before the season started and it went from there,' Brian continues. His debut could have come earlier. 'I'd been down to make my debut at Rotherham before they signed George Mulhall. If George hadn't signed I would have played. I travelled with the team.'

That had been almost a year earlier. Scotland international Mulhall had signed the previous September and since then hadn't missed a game. Mulhall was a left-winger, whereas Usher came into the team on the right and played all but the last of his 71 games for the club on the right. 'Actually, left-wing was my best position I think, but I didn't play there,' explains Brian. 'I could kick with both feet but when I first started playing school football I began at left-back and from then on until I made my debut as a right-winger I always played left side. I played left-wing in the youth team at Sunderland. I found it easier playing on the left wing because my stride pattern meant that I always ran off my left foot. This meant that if the ball came to me quickly on the left I was already into my stride.

'I didn't play more than the very odd game on the left wing until I joined Doncaster. I played there for George Raynor, who had managed Sweden to the final of the World Cup in 1958. He asked me which I preferred so I played on the left.' In between his time with Sunderland and Doncaster – where he still lives – Brian had played for his promotion-winning Sunderland manager Alan Brown at Sheffield Wednesday, but it was future Sunderland boss Lawrie McMenemy who continued with him on his chosen flank after taking over at Doncaster. 'I knew Lawrie from the north-east because he used to be coach at Gateshead and Bishop Auckland, and then he'd worked with Alan Brown at Sheffield Wednesday when I was at Hillsborough.'

Regardless of being on the 'wrong' wing, when he first came into the team at Sunderland Usher provided the sort of youthful energy that Gary Owers would do after making his debut on the opening day of the 1987/88 promotion season. Manager Brown had a simple instruction for young Brian: 'He always said to me, "Take them on. You won't get by every time but it's when you do that counts." That's what I like nowadays, to see wingers taking people on. There's plenty of space out there. These days you watch games and there's about 12 people in the penalty box. There's no room, but there's stacks on the wings.'

Three of the first four games were won before Brian got his first goal. It was the winner in a 1-0 victory at Bury – 'I didn't score a lot but I remember that one,' smiles Brian. 'It was played back to me as I was in the six-yard box.'

A week later a 2-0 home win over Manchester City took Sunderland into the promotion positions for the first time. Backing that up with another home victory against Scunthorpe, Brown's boys had dropped only three points (just two for a win then) from their opening eight games before the first blip of the season. Defeats at Swindon and Swansea – the latter in the League Cup – were followed by a couple of draws, but the start had been so good Sunderland were still second, two points behind early pacesetters Swindon.

Significantly, after the first of those draws at home to Cardiff Martin Harvey came into the team to replace the legendary Stan Anderson. The former skipper was controversially transferred to Newcastle but remained so popular he was warmly welcomed back to Roker for his own testimonial on the Monday before the final home game when promotion was finally sealed.

Colossal centre-half Charlie Hurley captained the side majestically. A towering presence at the back, 'King' Charlie was not the kind of defender who simply cleared the ball as far as he could kick it. The Republic of Ireland international liked to play constructively. In the early 60s he also set the tone for centre-halves going forward for corner kicks, something that is taken for granted now. Capped at international level as a centre-forward as well as at centre-half, Hurley created havoc whenever he went forward. Nippy centre-forward Nicky Sharkey always used to say he got a lot of his goals by being ready to pounce on rebounds from Hurley headers.

Charlie scored seven times in the promotion season. Two of his five league goals started and ended a sequence of four successive wins that took Sunderland to the top of the table. In between those Hurley-inspired victories at Norwich and at home to Plymouth Sunderland won two derby matches: one at Derby County and the other a real derby against Newcastle United.

Despite playing second division football, Sunderland averaged home gates of 41,258 over the season. 56,903 came through the doors to see a thunderbolt from left-back Len Ashurst equalise an early Newcastle goal by Colin Taylor. Derbies are often tense, scrappy affairs but this one was a rip-roaring game of football won for Sunderland nine minutes from time when George Herd fired home after George Mulhall threaded a pass across the box.

Inside-right Herd was one of Sunderland's finest footballers of the 60s. A clever technician, the Scotland international also possessed immense stamina. At times teams tried to man-mark him, but in this pre-substitute era when that happened George's policy was to just keep running all afternoon and then take advantage in the closing stages when the poor soul trying to keep up with him was worn out.

'Who could play with a better player than George Herd?' asks Usher, who linked with Herd on the right flank. 'At right-back big Cec [Irwin] would get the ball and give it to you early when the full-back was off you, so you had time to turn. If Cec played a ball up to me, all I had to do was play it inside and George Herd was there and he'd play it back to me inside the full-back. I'd just come into the team but all the players were good at helping me through games. They were smashing lads.'

Young Usher did so well that he was brought straight back into the side after missing his only competitive game of the campaign, despite Sunderland winning 4-1 in his absence. Tommy Mitchinson stood in for Brian as Leyton Orient were well beaten in mid-November – as he had 48 hours earlier when Sharkey struck a hat-trick in a friendly with Eusébio's Benfica where Sunderland won 5-3. But Brian was back in the number 7 shirt as Sunderland won at Swansea, the scene of their League Cup exit.

Brown stuck with Brian and indeed the rest of the team as just one game out of five was won following the trip to South Wales. The Saturday before Christmas brought a 5-1 loss on an icy pitch at Northampton where the team struggled in the wrong footwear. That wasn't the ideal preparation for the Christmas double-header with arch-rivals Leeds United.

Managed by Roker old boy Don Revie, Leeds were in the process of making enemies across the footballing world. Their rough play and gamesmanship – at a time when gamesmanship was largely yet to rear its ugly head – made them an unpopular club. As Sunderland stepped foot in Elland Road on Boxing Day, Leeds topped the table, three points ahead of second-placed Sunderland and with a game in hand.

In the final analysis both Leeds and Sunderland would go up, in that order. The following seasons would see Leeds become one of the dominant clubs in the country, while Sunderland struggled.

Losing manager Brown at the end of the season was a contributory factor in that. During the promotion campaign Sunderland would become involved in a demanding cup run that undoubtedly cost league points. Leeds would pip Sunderland to the title by two points but arguments over who was the better team of the two will always be open to debate. In the head-to-head Sunderland unquestionably came out on top.

At Leeds only a late equaliser from Ian Lawson protected United's unbeaten home record that they would carry through to the end of the season. In the return at Roker Park 24 hours later George Herd scored in the first minute and Nicky Sharkey doubled the lead before the game was a quarter of the way through. With over 55,000 inside Roker Park Leeds had the Roker Roar to contend with as well as the Lads as Sunderland triumphed 2-0.

Victory over Leeds sparked the best run of the season. It was the first of eight successive wins, five of these being in the league. Twelve goals were scored in two games, a 6-1 cup win over Bristol City and a 6-0 league triumph over one-time leaders Swindon, with Sharkey getting a hat-trick and Usher also hitting the mark.

By this time Sunderland topped the table but still had Leeds breathing down their necks. Revie's Leeds had been held at home by Cardiff as Swindon were being slaughtered at Sunderland to leave the Wearsiders a point ahead but having played a game more. Ultimately, what mattered most was not the distance between Sunderland and Leeds but the gap between Sunderland and the team in third place. That was Preston, who were just two points behind but like Leeds had a game in hand.

Having held Leeds at Elland Road, Cardiff might have fancied their chances of stopping Sunderland the following weekend, but goals from Mulhall and Sharkey eased the red and whites to a 2-0 win.

Sunderland were then in buoyant mood as they welcomed league champions Everton to Roker for an FA Cup fifth-round tie. The Toffees had eliminated Leeds in the fourth round but were blown away as Sunderland established a 3-0 half-time advantage and eventually won 3-1 in front of 62,851.

Cup fever could have damaged the promotion charge. The same regular XI were turning out week in, week out – and, of course, playing the full 90 minutes each time, often on heavy pitches. With an epic three games – plus two extra-time periods – to come against cup holders Manchester United in the quarter-final, ten of the regular XI played every cup game, left-half Jim McNab missing the Manchester United games through injury.

Sunderland led 3-1 with four minutes to go in the initial tie at Old Trafford, only to draw 3-3 following an injury to goalkeeper Jim Montgomery. United left it just as late in the replay, Bobby Charlton equalising in the last minute of extra time to force a second replay after a 2-2 draw.

Sunderland's record attendance of 75,118 is commonly believed to have been exceeded by many thousands that night according to many eyewitnesses. The official attendance was 10,000 fewer than the 56,675 who saw the Good Friday league game against Rotherham. Gates at both ends were broken down as the crowd clamoured for admission. The second replay saw Sunderland eventually well beaten at Huddersfield in a game sandwiched between league games with Middlesbrough and Newcastle in which just one point was gleaned by a tired team.

'I remember the games with Man U well,' recalls Brian Usher. 'We had already knocked out Everton who were the league champions. Had we beaten Man U I think we would have gone on to win the cup. We had special players like George Herd, George Mulhall and Charlie Hurley. They were as good as anybody.'

Defeat by a single goal on a wicked day at Newcastle, when many thought the game was to be postponed, was the only league reverse after Christmas. The result deposed Sunderland from the top of the table. On the same day Leeds leapfrogged Sunderland by winning at Middlesbrough. Preston remained hot on the heels of the top two. They were due to be the next visitors to Roker Park and by the time they got there were just a point behind after a comfortable midweek win over Norwich.

North End's visit sticks in Brian's memory: 'The game from the season that stands out has got to be the 4-0 win over Preston. They were third and we were second. We were 4-0 up by half-time. It was so important to win that game.'

Managed by Jimmy Milne (whose son Gordon managed Coventry in 1977 on the night of the scoreboard controversy as Sunderland were relegated), Preston were enjoying a cup run of their own and would reach the final. They put up stern resistance early on, but once Crossan opened the scoring in the 25th minute the floodgates opened as four goals came in 12 minutes. Mulhall and a couple from Sharkey put Sunderland in total control. The game did not secure promotion but it was a gigantic stride towards it.

After a win and a draw with Rotherham Usher notched the only goal of a home game with relegation-threatened Swansea. 'They always criticised the goalkeeper but I was always taught as a winger, "When you get near the line, smash it!" This was because you had forwards running in and defenders running back and anything could happen. It might have been a fluke but it did what I intended it to do. I hit it hard and low and it went in.'

With the finishing line in sight Sunderland won 5-2 at Leyton Orient and took a point from a goalless draw at Southampton to go into the final home game against fourth-placed Charlton Athletic needing a point (from their last two games) to be mathematically certain of a first-ever promotion. Given the frustratingly narrow near misses of the previous two seasons nerves jangled as the Addicks took an early lead, but George Herd levelled just before half-time. Former Sunderland goalkeeper Peter Wakeham produced an outstanding display to try and thwart his old team-mates, but a minute from time top scorer Johnny Crossan settled matters by making it 2-1 to take away any worries of conceding a late winner.

Sunderland were up. It was a feeling never experienced before. Before the war there had been six league titles and an FA Cup triumph but post-war only promises and broken dreams. For war babies like Brian Usher it was the first time the club had achieved anything in their lifetime. 'I remember running around the field with big Charlie and everybody,' he says of the lap of honour. 'I think it's everybody's ambition when they join a club to get into the first team and then hope for the best. It was the first time it was ever done because they had never been out of the first division until 1958.

'I was from Easington Lane. My dad worked at the pit at Elemore and then he got transferred to Murton when that closed. I used to live at the Brick Garth. It was terrific playing at Roker Park. I supported Sunderland as a boy. There were about six of us used to leave at about 11 o'clock on a Saturday morning when they were at home. We'd get to Park Lane on the bus and then make our way over to the ground. I used to watch players like Billy Bingham, Billy Elliott, Charlie Fleming, Ted Purdon and Ken Chisholm. It was a terrific place, Sunderland. It was the one team that I played for that I wished I could have been good enough to stop there but it wasn't to be.'

Brian scored Sunderland's final goal of the season in a 2-2 draw at Grimsby, who went down after failing to win. He then got on the scoresheet twice more, in a testimonial at Hartlepool and at Linfield in the final game of a three-match end-of-season tour of Ireland.

After being just one game short of joining Jim Montgomery, Len Ashurst, Johnny Crossan and George Mulhall as an ever-present in the promotion team, Brian went on to play 20 times in the top flight before being sold to Sheffield Wednesday for £18,000 in the summer of 1965.

Promotion-winning manager Alan Brown had joined Wednesday after leaving Sunderland following the promotion win, having had a disagreement with the directors who refused to let him purchase his club-owned house at a preferential rate. At Hillsborough Usher vied with future Sunderland manager Howard Wilkinson for the right-wing berth. In his second season in Sheffield he played in a big 5-0 Hillsborough win against his old club, while his third year with the Owls was his best, a highlight being a goal in a 1-1 draw against Manchester United at a time Wednesday were third in the league.

Nonetheless, Brian Usher's proudest moments in football were as a young local lad who came into the team at the right time and became part of that never-to-be-forgotten side: Montgomery, Irwin, Ashurst, Harvey, Hurley, McNab, Usher, Herd, Sharkey, Crossan and Mulhall.

1975/76 DIVISION TWO CHAMPIONS

*Dick Malone had been an FA Cup winner with
Sunderland in 1972/73 and remained at the club
as a second trophy was won under Bob Stokoe in
a season which could easily have been a promotion
and cup double.*

WHEREAS THE first promotion team's regular XI can be recited by many of the supporters still around who watched them, many of the regulars of this second promotion side are forgotten by many, despite the fact that the 1976 side were champions while the class of '64 were runners-up.

Why is this? The 1964 team remain revered and as time passes and several of them pass away, each death creates a crater-sized impact in the psyche of the support. The 1976 team simply does not carry the same hold on supporters. Not that there wasn't delight and elation when the promotion arrived.

It had been longed for but it took too long. The time out of the top flight was the same as the '64 team suffered – six years. The difference was that halfway through this second division sojourn Sunderland won the FA Cup. Fans and players alike were desperate to see that cup-winning team unleashed on the first division. After all they hadn't just beaten Leeds to win the trophy, they had knocked out Arsenal and Manchester City – three of the country's top teams

– and then added another top contemporary scalp early the following term by defeating 1972 (and 1975) champions Derby County after three pulsating games in the League Cup.

Some quality players had come in. Former Scotland captain Bob Moncur arrived from Newcastle and did for Sunderland what Stan Anderson had done for the Magpies just over a decade earlier, i.e. inspire to promotion the club that had been his local rivals while becoming a hero on the other half of the Wear–Tyne divide. Another ex-Newcastle man was Bryan 'Pop' Robson, outrageously never capped by England despite being the top flight's top scorer when with West Ham in the season Sunderland were cup winners. Someone who did win England caps after starring in the Roker midfield was Tony Towers. Centre-half Jeff Clarke had also been signed, like Towers, from Man City, while left-back Joe Bolton had come through the ranks and was on the way to achieving cult hero status.

After missing the opening two games of the season, right-back Dick Malone missed just one more – and that after promotion was secured. A key part of the FA Cup-winning side three years earlier, obviously that legendary achievement outstrips the promotion win but why does Dick believe winning Division Two under Bob Stokoe is largely forgotten?

'I've never thought about that but you're right. It does get overlooked completely because all anyone wants to talk about is the cup. To be fair, at the time the cup was the best competition in the world and the way we won it, which was against probably three of the best teams in Europe, I think that is why. The team changed and you've got fans who have got the names of the 1973 cup team printed into their brain but they don't really relate to the '75/76 season. To be honest I'm the same as them. I don't think of the '75/76 season, which is stupid. There doesn't seem to be any glamour about the 1975/76 team.'

Glamour had evaporated with the break-up of the cup-winning side. Goalkeeper Jim Montgomery and the right flank of Malone and Bobby Kerr were still intact, none of the trio missing more than four games, but otherwise there were just remnants of the cup side. Centre-forward Vic Halom played in every game bar one up to Christmas but only three afterwards. Wembley goalscorer Ian Porterfield signed off just before Christmas in the same game where Halom ceased to be a regular, Ian's last game being at Chelsea who he would later manage. Meanwhile, Billy Hughes had a run of ten starts in the autumn but otherwise was very much on the fringe of the team.

The other five members of the starting XI at Wembley were no longer at the club. Ritchie Pitt had suffered a cruel career-ending injury before Dennis Tueart and Micky Horswill went to Manchester City, which later also became the destination of Dave Watson, while the ageing Ron Guthrie had dropped into non-league. 'I think at the time Micky and Dennis were transferred they left the club basically for pennies. At the time of the cup final Micky was on £25 a week and £25 appearance money and all he was after was parity with the rest of the players which was nowt really, and Dennis wanted a few bob extra as well. Bob [Stokoe] was fantastic. I argued regularly with him but we got on really well. He wasn't strong enough with the directors really and it allowed the team to break up. When you've got an engine that's running well, if you tinker with it you ruin all the timing and that's exactly what happened.'

Sunderland were evidently a good side in 1975/76. Winning the league illustrates this but they were more like an efficient family saloon rather than the Rolls-Royce they had been in the cup year.

The season began with a crowd of just under 29,000 witnessing a 2-1 win over Chelsea, a trademark clinically finished goal from Pop Robson being the first of 67 that made Sunderland the division's top scorers. After a chastening 3-0 midweek defeat at Bristol City, Malone and Monty came into the side, Jackie Ashurst and Trevor Swinburne having worn the number 2 and 1 shirts in the opening games. After a 1-1 draw at Oxford where Bob Moncur came up with a second-half equaliser, the next two games at Roker brought victories that maintained a 100 per cent home record. In the first of that pair against Fulham, debutant Mel Holden opened the scoring with Tommy Gibb – an ex-Magpie opening-day debutant – also on the mark.

Holden had impressed against Sunderland the previous September. He had led the line for third division Preston alongside player-manager Bobby Charlton and future England international Tony Morley in a League Cup tie where a Sunderland team including seven 1973 Wembley heroes, plus players of the calibre of Moncur, Towers and Robson, were lucky to lose only 2-0. Preston were fabulous that night. Holden went on to be their top scorer with 23 goals and when Stokoe paid £120,000 for the 20-year-old it looked like an astute acquisition.

Holden was always a gangly and at times awkward-looking player but he was a great foil for poacher Pop Robson. In the final analysis when promotion was won Mel's dozen league goals were only one fewer than Robson who had started nine more games, albeit Holden had come off the bench five times. For good measure the pair each scored three more in cup ties.

After his debut goal Holden waited two and a half months for another in the league. During this spell he had a period where he was left on the bench for four consecutive games but come the end of the season – at a time when there was just one sub – he had been named in the matchday 12 for every game.

By the time he got back on the Division Two scoresheet Sunderland were setting the pace. Holden's brace secured a win at Charlton that was a fourth successive victory. The previous week Vic Halom had scored twice in a 3-0 home win over Nottingham Forest. They were the last goals scored for the club by the 1973 cup-winning centre-forward.

Having come off the bench to score his brace at Charlton – in a match refereed by Jack Taylor who had refereed the previous World Cup Final – Holden went on to start every game bar one – when he came on as sub at Chelsea – until the end of the season. After promotion Mel managed nine goals in 24 top-flight games, a pretty decent record, especially in a side that (gallantly) went down. He would play his final game for the club in January 1978 after which he briefly played for Blackpool. He then switched to Holland with PEC Zwolle shortly after their first-ever promotion to the Dutch top flight, the Eredivisie. Tragically, that young centre-forward who people had felt was gangly and ungainly at Sunderland died at the age of just 26, a victim of motor neurone disease. Three years and three days before his death he had been playing for Sunderland at Cardiff. This illness had forced Mel to retire from playing a year after leaving Wearside.

By the time poor Mel Holden passed away Sunderland had been relegated and promoted again. In the season of 1975/76 when Holden was a massively influential figure in Sunderland's promotion, following his two goals at Charlton in November Sunderland stayed top of the table for a couple of months when a defeat at Fulham briefly saw them overtaken by Bolton and Bristol City.

By this time the FA Cup run had started. Four days before the loss at Craven Cottage Hull had been beaten in a fourth-round tie at Roker, Holden having scored in a third-round victory over Oldham. The Saturday after the Fulham failure Sunderland travelled to top-flight Stoke City. The Potters were in the top half of the table and Sunderland's away record of three wins, three draws and seven defeats was less than might be expected of a promotion-chasing side. With a typically big away support, over 41,000 packed into the Victoria Ground (Stoke's biggest gate of the season despite having Man City and Spurs at home in the previous two rounds) to see Sunderland come away with a goalless draw.

Over 47,000 came to Roker for the replay in which goals from Holden and Robson overcame Stoke's reply from future Sunderland promotion-winning manager Denis Smith. Mel and Pop were among the scorers again three days later as Charlton were thrashed 4-1 with Holden again on the mark next time out in a draw at Carlisle, but as the cup quarter-final loomed there was defeat at Luton.

The cup quarter-final brought third division Crystal Palace to Sunderland. Hopes were high of emulating the cup success of only three years earlier. Up to this point only Bristol Rovers had taken a point from Roker where three teams had also seen their cup hopes ended. Indeed, over the whole season only two points were dropped at home. With over 50,000 expectant fans in the ground Palace boss Malcolm Allison came on to the pitch pre-match, lapping up the abuse of the Fulwell End as he waved his fedora hat at them. Allison had been in charge of Manchester City when they had lost to Sunderland in the fifth-round replay in 1973.

It wasn't Allison, Palace, or even infamous referee Clive Thomas who proved to be Sunderland's biggest opponent that afternoon. It was the wind – the same North Sea gale that blew Sunderland off course against Chelsea when promotion was there for the taking in 1963. The team of '76 – like the team of '64 almost did – could so easily have made it a promotion and cup double. As in the previous promotion year the quarter-final was reached.

'The cup game against Crystal Palace sticks in my mind because we should have won,' declares Dick. 'We missed quite a few chances and they had one breakaway and scored. That's when Arthur [coach Arthur Cox] got the sack. I don't know how they could sack him. Arthur was the reason Sunderland were doing well. He was first class. He knew everything about the game psychologically. He motivated the players. Everything was half full. You never had down moments when Arthur was about. At times Bob's chin could be on the deck but Arthur was the shining light. Bob was great as well. I'm making it sound as if Bob did nothing but he was a good manager to have, but he needed someone like Arthur to back him up and keep everything on a level, an even keel. Where he made the mistake was appointing Ian MacFarlane because I don't believe he was the right solution to the problem.'

Cox performed a similar role to Viv Busby and Bobby Saxton in the forthcoming chapters on the 1987/88, 1989/90 and 1998/99 promotions. Well liked by the players, he kept spirits up, provided a few laughs despite his dour reputation and played a leading role in simply getting the team to play well.

Featuring future Sunderland forward Dave Swindlehurst and Ian 'Taff' Evans, who later came to Sunderland as Mick McCarthy's assistant, Palace hung on and scored the only goal of the game 14 minutes from time through former Everton striker Alan Whittle. Going out of the cup was a disappointment. Palace fell to Lawrie McMenemy's Southampton in the semi-final as the Saints went on to emulate Stokoe's stars of '73 by winning the FA Cup while in the second division. Sunderland's aim, of course, was to get out of the second division, but while the response to going out of the cup was good – a Bobby Kerr brace bringing an away win at Orient –

victory at Brisbane Road was the only one in a spell of six games either side of the cup quarter-final. Perhaps Kerr was responding to the signing of debutant Ray Train, like Kerr a busily industrious midfielder, who at 5ft 5in towered a whole inch above the cup-winning skipper. 'Ray Train was a little workhorse and he was a good player,' remembers Malone.

In the aftermath of the cup defeat coach Cox was replaced by Ian MacFarlane who had previously worked at Roker (and Sheffield Wednesday) under Alan Brown. Writing in the first *Roker Review* match programme after the change Doug Weatherall wrote, 'The booming Big Man [MacFarlane] is wonderful company in or out of a dressing room. I have yet to meet a player who does not love being under his wing.'

Dick Malone did not share Doug's opinion: 'I think they sacked Arthur Cox after the Malcolm Allison team beat us 1-0 in the cup. Soon after Bob phoned Arthur and apologised to him. He said, "I think I've made a big mistake. I've lost the dressing room." And that's when everything started to crumble.'

While promotion was won, before two months of the following season had elapsed Stokoe resigned. The second of the two trophies he brought to the club was freshly on display. Malone and MacFarlane didn't see eye to eye. 'I used to tell Ian MacFarlane about his language. We would be in hotels with young girls serving, and his language was atrocious. I couldn't get it out of my head that could be my daughter he was talking to. I thought, "What a foul '20-stone' canary" he was – because he wore a bright yellow tracksuit.'

There were to be further problems between the two when MacFarlane took over as caretaker manager in the autumn, but at the time of MacFarlane's appointment there was promotion to be won. On the Saturday before the FA Cup semi-finals the team Sunderland's cup conquerors Palace were due to meet at Stamford Bridge – Southampton – came to Roker. Perhaps they had one eye on their semi-final but they were no match for the Lads who cantered to a 3-0 win with two goals from Roy Greenwood, a wiry winger who had signed in January for just £5,000 less than the £145,000 spent on Pop Robson a year and a half earlier.

'Roy Greenwood had pace and was a lovely guy,' says Malone. 'He was a decent player but could be a bit timid and if there was a strong challenge against him his game could suffer a little bit I thought.'

Those goals against Southampton were Greenwood's only strikes in the 16 games of the promotion season following his mid-season move. He helped earn the trophy but not a place on the following season's team photo as apparently Stokoe wouldn't allow him on it as he had a beard. Nonetheless, Bobby Kerr, Tommy Gibb and Mel Holden all appeared sporting moustaches that were evidently decreed acceptable!

The bearded winger's goals against McMenemy's men started a decisive run where only one point was dropped in six games. The penultimate fixture of that sequence saw Gary Rowell score his first-ever goal in a 4-1 win at Greenwood's old club Hull, with the following match being the one where promotion was secured.

51,983 came to Roker Park for what was an Easter Monday meeting with Bolton Wanderers. Going into the match where there were still two points for a win, Sunderland were four points ahead of Bolton with each having three games to play. In between, Bristol City and West Brom were one and two points respectively behind Stokoe's men but each had played a game more.

'There was a bit of pressure there,' remembers Dick of a day when the visitors included three men who would go on to play major roles at Sunderland: Barry Siddall, Peter Reid and Sam Allardyce. 'What really put the cat amongst the pigeons was when Big Sam headed the ball in the net but fortunately we managed to hold on at the death,' reflects Malone. Sunderland had settled nerves with a 2-0 half-time lead provided by a Tony Towers penalty and Pop Robson, but 12 minutes from the end Allardyce scored with a header as he had done in the reverse fixture at Christmas. 'We played reasonably well but all I can remember is we shouldn't have been in that position anyway. We should have had it sewn up long before. We lost a few stupid games.'

Robson's promotion-winning goal was his 13th and final league goal of the season, a tally that made him top scorer, although he had scored six more the previous term and would score 20 when promotion was won again four years later. 'Pop was Pop. No matter where he went he scored goals,' says Dick. 'Pop was great in the 18-yard box but the fluency of the team had parted. It was disappointing. Billy [Hughes] had had the break in his leg but he was back by that time, although he had lost a yard of pace so he was on the borderline of the team every week. Sometimes he played but if I remember rightly, most times he didn't play. It was flat. Dave Watson had gone. The cup team had broken up. It was ridiculous. The directors did nothing to help us at all. After we won the cup the wage freeze was on but they could have done something. Titles could have been changed and we could have got a rise.'

Given the three-year post-Wembley search for promotion, when the place in the top flight was secured was it more a case of relief that what people had long expected had been achieved? 'Yes.' Dick pauses to consider and continues. 'Yes. I think it was a bit of relief, and excitement as well. The relief being the fact that it was expected of us and it was getting to the stage where the fans were getting a bit frustrated.'

Malone, Monty and Bobby Kerr were rested 24 hours later for a game at mid-table Blackpool which was lost 1-0, before relegated Portsmouth sportingly provided a guard of honour at Roker Park where goals from Joe Bolton and Billy Hughes ensured Sunderland didn't just win promotion but the Division Two trophy.

Testimonial matches at home to Leeds and away to Newcastle for Bobby Kerr and future Sunderland promotion-winning assistant manager Frank Clark were then played but the season was still not over. Having played 51 league and cup games as well as a mid-season joint testimonial for injury victims Ritchie Pitt and Bobby Park, after the Kerr and Clark benefits the squad embarked on a ten-match southern hemisphere tour that stretched into June.

'In the background I kept thinking, "We're on this bloody tour now, for over six weeks,"' says Dick of a trip that saw games in Tahiti, New Zealand and six separate states in Australia and Singapore. 'We were flying, training and playing. I didn't touch a drop of alcohol but some of the players were getting bladdered and getting rests. I played in every game. I was the idiot. When I came home I sat in the chair and fell asleep sitting up and never flinched for five hours. The first ten days of the tour I only had ten hours' sleep. I couldn't get to sleep. We were crossing the international dateline. Oh God … that worried me, going on tour after winning promotion. There were so many flights. When the season started back, everyone was knackered and we were as flat as anything. That probably contributed to a lot of the players that had gone on that tour not fulfilling their normal game during that season.'

The opening friendly for that season took place at the end of the following month after the return from the tour, after which a tour of Scandinavia and a home friendly preceded a start to the season which saw ten league games played before a win was registered. By the time a Division One victory was achieved Stokoe had resigned, leaving MacFarlane in caretaker charge.

The opening three league games had been drawn when Malone and Montgomery missed a 4-1 defeat at Bristol City. After another loss at Middlesbrough Dick and Jim were restored but after losing at home to Manchester City and drawing at Manchester United in the League Cup Malone was left out again. 'Bob called me in and apologised to me. He said, "I don't like saying this to anyone. Especially not my best and most consistent player," and that's fact, "but I'm leaving you out for the games." I said, "Are you joking?"' Understandably Dick sounds incredulous while recalling this and explains, 'He said, "I promised when Ian MacFarlane came to give him his head."'

The tie with Manchester United went to two replays. The second of those would be the last Malone played for Stokoe (as well as Jim Montgomery's 627th and final appearance for the club). Malone didn't feature in MacFarlane's first game after Stokoe left but was restored after a defeat at QPR. Dick played in a win at Coventry, a 1-0 defeat at reigning champions Liverpool and a thrilling 3-3 draw on a foggy night at Manchester United officiated by 1973 cup final ref Ken Burns. Despite his role in that improvement that saw the Lads climb off the bottom of the table, Malone was again dropped and didn't play again until MacFarlane's reign was over.

Promotion had come and quickly gone for the remaining members of the team of '73. Malone would only play twice for new manager Jimmy Adamson and with Billy Hughes playing his final game soon afterwards, only Bobby Kerr of the cup winners remained as the season ended in immediate relegation. Of the eight times Sunderland have been promoted to the top flight this was the first of four occasions when they went straight back down!

Malone still has his cup winners' medal but didn't get a medal for winning the league: 'We got a shield with the winners on it. I'd rather have had a medal. They're better and look better when you're showing someone and telling the story behind it.' Evidently, there was quite a story to tell of a promotion where the seeds of immediate relegation seem to have been sown before the team even went up. Perhaps that's why the 1976 team seems to not have the same hold on supporters' – and perhaps players' – memories.

1979/80 DIVISION TWO RUNNERS-UP

Having narrowly missed out on promotion a year earlier Sunderland made no mistake, clinching promotion by defeating West Ham United two days after the Hammers had won the FA Cup. Capped by England B at Roker Park during the promotion season, Shaun Elliott recollects the promotion under Ken Knighton.

PROMOTION IN 1980 came after four years out of the top flight – two fewer than in the previous spells out of the top level. Sunderland had finished just two points off the top spot a year earlier in 1978/79, but that was enough to miss out in a tight table as gigantic support on the last day at Wrexham waited for news of other results after Sunderland had beaten the Welsh side. Rivals Stoke and Brighton had both won – Brighton at Newcastle. The thousands who gave Wrexham a gate over 11,000 larger than their next home game two days later travelled home (me on the back of a motorbike to Sheffield, where I was a student, after sleeping in and missing the Doncaster SAFC supporters' branch bus!) with Sunderland still in a promotion position. The scenario was that, as in 1964 with Chelsea, a London team still had a game to play. This time it was Crystal Palace who duly beat Burnley to squeeze Sunderland out of the promotion frame.

The Lads had done well under caretaker manager Billy Elliott who had taken over before Christmas. It was a surprise when the Sunderland star of the 50s and trainer to the 1973 cup team was passed over in favour of 35-year-old first-team coach Ken Knighton, who was appointed manager. 'It was a difficult one,' says Shaun Elliott, who missed just one game of both the promotion season and the narrow miss under Elliott. 'At the time when Ken was appointed my recollection of it was that all the managers who came to Sunderland were well-known people. When Ken came that sort of bucked the trend. I wasn't familiar with him at all before he arrived as coach and I suppose the majority of the team weren't. He was a pleasant enough guy although at the end we didn't see eye to eye I suppose. He brought Frank Clark in with him and that didn't help in that he was a Newcastle player through and through, but everything went well. We just had a few issues at the end.' Knighton had to take the step from coach to manager at a time when he was less than a couple of years older than his senior player (Pop Robson). 'It's always a difficult scenario,' says Shaun. 'It's a lot different when you're in the hot seat but there has to be a dividing line.'

The season began with a decent point from a goalless draw at newly relegated Chelsea, before Robson got the first goal of the campaign to open the scoring in a 2-0 home win over Birmingham City. Having been top scorer in the previous promotion team Robson had been re-signed in the summer from West Ham and would go on to be way out in front as the club's top scorer, as he fired Sunderland back to the top flight with 20 goals from 40 league games.

'Pop was a huge, huge influence on me from being a kid,' Elliott explains. 'We're from the same area. He based himself in Hexham and he took me under his wing as such. When I signed as a professional we ended up travelling in together as much as we could. That was great for me. He was a seasoned pro and taught me everything about life when I was a young kid being thrust into the limelight as such. I was just on the verge of the first team. He even talked to me about things like pensions; he was like a father figure to me and I always looked up to him as everybody did. He was underestimated as a player. He was as sharp as a tack. Pop would always be in my best XI as a goalscorer.'

Robson netted the winner in the next game against Fulham with a penalty, but after dropping just one point from the opening three games there was just one win from the next five. This could actually be said to be one win from seven given that the same run saw both legs of a League Cup tie finish 2-2. This resulted in Sunderland's first-ever penalty shoot-out where Newcastle were beaten at St James'. First division Manchester City were then beaten in a replay with a goal from Robson before the run ended in November in another replay at West Ham.

By this stage the table was shaping up and Sunderland were far from front runners. Two days before the League Cup loss at the Boleyn Ground a home win over Chelsea had marked the one-third point of the season. Knighton's red and whites were tenth with a five-point gap to leaders Luton at a time when it was still two points for a win. Newcastle were one of four teams in joint second place on 18 points.

Knighton was certainly being backed by chairman Keith Collings. Popular goalkeeper Barry Siddall was replaced as Knighton installed his new signing Chris Turner, who he knew from one of his old clubs Sheffield Wednesday. Sunderland's record transfer fee of £200,000 was then equalled with the purchase of centre-forward John Hawley, who Knighton knew from their time at Hull. Perhaps encouraged by seeing Hawley hit a hat-trick on his league debut as Charlton were smashed 4-0 at Roker, Collings flourished the chequebook to break the club's transfer record twice before Christmas. £300,000 went to Middlesbrough for Stan Cummins in November, and after the diminutive winger scored in his first two games a fee of £380,000 was agreed the following month with Argentinian club San Lorenzo for midfielder Claudio Marangoni. Knighton had been keen to follow the trend of bringing in players from Argentina, who had won the FIFA World Cup the previous year. In the summer he had gone close to signing Alex Sabella from Sheffield United for what would have trebled the club-record fee.

In mid-October Elliott had been one of the scorers in a 5-2 friendly win over Paraguayan side Olimpia Asuncion on a night when Sunderland fielded two Argentinians – Hordon Palmeira and

Ruben Alcides Giordano – as triallists. A couple of years earlier Sunderland had even become the first overseas team to try and sign Diego Maradona, only for Argentina's military rulers to thwart plans for their top young talent to be exported at that time.

Despite the pressures of a promotion season the meeting with the Paraguayans wasn't the only autumn friendly. In November 1979 Sunderland also entertained an England XI as the club celebrated its centenary, losing to two goals from Everton's Bob Latchford. Given the need to win promotion and the fact that there had been six hard-fought games in the League Cup, Sunderland weren't shy about entering an extra competition.

It seems strange to contemplate now but on the Wednesday night before a league game at Orient Sunderland fielded five of their best players in what was then the prestigious *Daily Express* five-a-side tournament at Wembley Arena. 'It was a big thing,' remembers Elliott. 'It was strange because we'd gone to London and people were wondering, "Do we want to play in this before a big game?" A lot of people were thinking, "We'll swerve this – I don't really want to play," but anyway the team was chosen and we just went on and on and got further until we won it. That was a cracking five-a-side team. Little Stan was wonderful up front and then you had Mick Buckley and Kevin Arnott plus myself and then Chris Turner in goal. It really was a good team. We were playing on the boards which weren't as smooth as how they appear on TV, trust me. We were all there, all the team and back-room staff. Peter Eustace was in charge of the team that night so there was just Peter on the photographs along with Cookie [youngster John Cooke] who was the sub, and the physio.'

Ipswich and West Brom were each beaten 2-0, with the same scoreline settling the final against Brighton. The semi-final had seen Newcastle walloped 4-0 meaning that in the calendar year of 1979 Sunderland had scored a grand total of 19 goals against the Magpies, including the Wembley tournament and the cup penalty shoot-out!

While it was nice to have become the first Sunderland team to win at Wembley (albeit the arena, not the stadium!) since Stokoe's stars of 1973, the trophy win didn't help the league campaign as the following Saturday Sunderland lost at Orient, a team who had lost their previous home match 7-3 to Chelsea. At this point Sunderland were eighth in the table, six points adrift of joint leaders Chelsea and Newcastle and with no play-offs in existence.

The Brisbane Road beating would be the last of 1979 as the rest of December went well. The best league gate since August saw the next game as Marangoni debuted in a home win over Cardiff. Following a draw at Watford the South American scored on his second appearance at Roker as Shrewsbury were beaten, but while local lad Cummins had become an instant hit Marangoni failed to excite. These days overseas players are routinely perceived to need a season or so to acclimatise, but Claudio was expected to leave the summer of his own country for a Wearside winter, a totally different kind of football, and immediately turn on the style. He did well to score in three of his first nine games from midfield but didn't fulfil expectations and within a year was back in South America, where he went on to play for Argentina and win the continent's top trophies.

He was certainly out of his comfort zone on New Year's Day as despite Stan Cummins providing the lead Sunderland slumped to a 3-1 loss at league leaders Newcastle. The result was hardly a surprise given Sunderland's poor away form – Marangoni's winner at Fulham four days earlier had brought the first league away win of the season, while Newcastle had dropped only one point at St James'.

The Magpies, however, fell away, winning only two of their remaining 18 games – and losing to a Cummins goal at Roker at Easter. In contrast, after going out of the FA Cup, the following weekend Sunderland stormed to promotion. Cup elimination to Bolton was a coupon buster. The Trotters didn't win away all season as they were relegated from the top flight, while Sunderland were unbeaten at home in the league all season in winning promotion – cue a 1-0 home loss to a team including Peter Reid and Sam Allardyce.

The response to losing the derby and the cup tie was magnificent. There was to be just one more defeat in the remaining 18 games and none at all in the final 14 from the moment left-back Joe Hinnigan debuted in February.

Modern-day managers often grumble about fixture overload and this in an era where squad rotation and the possibility of up to five subs a game can share the workload on usually pristine pitches. Back in 1980 in the days of only one sub, Sunderland played three games in four days at Easter, won them all and went to the top of the table for the first time. Away wins at Wrexham and Shrewsbury followed the Good Friday beating of Newcastle.

Leaders at last, it was certainly tight at the top. Birmingham City and Chelsea were level with the Lads on 47 points, Knighton's men top by a single goal with Leicester and Luton close behind. Draws in the next two games made the third to last game at home to Watford a must-win. Equalling the biggest victory of the season – when Cummins got four in a 5-0 win over Burnley in February – Robson and Elliott bagged a brace each with Buckley also on the scoresheet. 'I remember the goals but there was something else in that game which nobody seems to remember,' says Shaun. 'I scored a goal in that game from a corner but it was disallowed because the referee said Pop Robson was pushing somebody. I would have had a hat-trick but one of my best mates had pushed somebody – and Pop isn't big enough to push anybody.'

The final away game saw Sunderland's vast travelling support give Cardiff a gate over 10,000 higher than for their recent home game with Newcastle. In what was a 1-1 draw, Sunderland dropped more than a point. Centre-half Jeff Clarke had been a rock at the heart of defence all season. Injury had ruled him out of the climax of the campaign in the previous promotion season four seasons earlier and at Ninian Park a broken leg saw him stretchered off.

Just as Niall Quinn and Kevin Phillips are the best attacking partnership I've seen in over half a century of watching Sunderland, Jeff Clarke and Shaun Elliott are the best defensive duo I've seen. Were they as good as Dave Watson and Charlie Hurley? Not as individuals but Watson and King Charlie never played together. Jeff and Shaun perfectly complemented each other. Clarke was a colossus who commanded the air. Shaun was the speed merchant who would not be beaten for pace. He was also excellent in the air if he needed to be, although when partnered with Clarke he'd usually be the covering defender and he was so good on the ball that he could bring it out of defence without making the crowd panic.

'I was lucky enough to play with Jeff who was a great player,' says Shaun, who still keeps in touch with his old mate. 'He came in exchange for Dave Watson who had gone to Man City. He suffered badly from injuries to his knees which was difficult because he's a big guy and it was difficult for him to turn. For him to get through his career was a miracle. One of those injuries finished Cloughie off and Jeff had two of them and still finished his career. That speaks volumes for his character as well and I was lucky enough to play with him as a fantastic central defence partner.'

Playing in central defence was Elliott's best position but with Sunderland also having the excellent young Rob Hindmarch, who played 21 times in the promotion season, and Gordon Chisholm also capable of playing centre-half, Shaun was often shunted into midfield. He explains, 'I always considered myself to be a centre-half. When I first came as a kid, I came as a centre-forward. I was never a centre-forward. I mean, I was okay but it wasn't until Martin Harvey had a big say that I started playing centre-half. I quickly developed in the reserves and went on to the first team as a centre-half. Around that time with various managers – because I was adaptable and I had some of the traits which would work in midfield – a lot of them wanted to play me in midfield and that ended up causing a little bit of bad feeling because I didn't want to play there. I wanted to be a centre-half. That was my strongest position. Ken Knighton liked to play me in midfield and so did other managers. I remember when I went to America [Elliott spent the summer of 1981 playing for Seattle Sounders] Alan Durban got the job and the first time I walked into the dressing room – I'd just got back the day before, and I was a bit jet-lagged but there was a game at Roker and I went down – the first thing he said to me was, "Ah, here's my midfield dynamo" and I thought, "Oh f***!" I thought this isn't going to go well and Alan and myself didn't get on. It wasn't anything against him. He just wanted me to play in midfield and I didn't like playing in midfield so we were never going to be best buddies.'

Five years later Elliott missed the League Cup Final through suspension and still feels for Clarke that he missed the promotion clincher against West Ham. 'It was Jeff's cup final because we were to be playing at Roker Park in front of 47,000 to win promotion. That was one of the best days of my life.' West Ham had beaten Arsenal in the FA Cup Final two days before the Monday night match at Roker, where the gates were closed long before kick-off with thousands locked out.

Sunderland needed a point to go up on goal difference but the newly crowned cup holders were obviously a very good side. Thankfully they had spent the weekend celebrating their Wembley triumph. 'I remember seeing them when they walked in and they actually looked as if they'd been celebrating for the last couple of days but it was all about our application as well. We had a great defensive unit. We didn't give a lot of goals away and playing at Roker the fans were going nuts because they knew what was going to happen. My mental attitude was I thought they'd been on the booze for two days now and it's going to wear off at some stage. They were very strong for the first half an hour but they ran out of a little bit of steam. Our application was that it was here for us to win and I just mentally had it on that whatever we do we're not giving away an early goal, which was my mentality in every game – we do not give goals away!'

Since the Cardiff game Sunderland had played a testimonial for Mick Docherty against QPR, managed by his father Tommy, who had managed the Chelsea team which put a spanner in Sunderland's promotion hopes in 1963. However, there had still been a full week of preparation which paid off as goals from Kevin Arnott, shortly before half-time, and a Cummins cracker midway through the second half got the promotion party started. 'I've still got photographs in my little den of that night and of me spraying champagne on people. Pop was in it and reporters and photographers were in the dressing room as well.'

Sunderland were promoted as runners-up, a point behind champions Leicester and ahead of Birmingham on goal difference. Whereas in 1963 Chelsea edged Sunderland out of the frame by winning after Sunderland's fixture list was complete, this time the Roker win over the Hammers meant Chelsea missed out on goal difference.

Unfortunately, for some diehard supporters the rearranged game with West Ham meant they missed the big night. Sunderland had organised an end-of-season trip to the USA with supporters able to book to join them by way of making it more affordable for the club. Those supporters left by coach to the airport for the scheduled flights on the morning of the promotion decider with the players rebooked to follow after the game. Forty-eight hours after beating West Ham Arnott scored again in Miami as Fort Lauderdale Strikers were beaten 2-1.

Playing around the world is something Elliott should have done more of, regardless of spending the following summer with Seattle.

In March of the promotion season he had won the first of his three England B caps against Spain at Roker Park. Many think he should have had a full cap. 'I loved the game. We played Spain and it was nice to play with top-class people,' says Shaun. 'I'm not being derogatory to the boys I usually played with but these players were internationals for a reason. Pop should certainly have been capped, as should Jeff Clarke. For me …', there is an extremely long pause while he considers, '… I was good but whether I was good enough to get an England cap is another matter. It's not for me to say. All I think is that people like Alvin Martin got capped and I certainly had the edge on him. Deep down I felt that Ossie – Russell Osman – was a bit better than me plus he was playing with Lofty – Terry Butcher – at club level, so it made sense for Russell Osman and Terry Butcher to play together for England a lot of the time. I don't think I was far off being as good as Russ but Russ was probably slightly better than me. I was quicker than Russell and I had two half-decent feet, whereas he was a little bit stockier than me. Was he better than me in the air? I don't know. It's a funny one for debate but given some of the people who did get caps, if you're asking me if I'm disappointed I didn't get a full cap, the answer would be yes. I think when we were around there was always a dividing line with the southern guys.'

A tremendous player who appeared over 300 times for Sunderland, Shaun Elliott was definitely good enough to play for England and unlucky to miss the 1985 League Cup Final when he would have captained the side, so being a key part of the 1980 promotion team goes down as the highlight of what was a terrific career by a class player.

1987/88 DIVISION THREE CHAMPIONS

Paul 'Jack' Lemon was never the darling of the crowd but was a hard-working member of Denis Smith's side who bounced back immediately after a first-ever relegation to the third tier. Lemon scored nine goals in 35+6 league games as he played his part in what became a successful season.

THE DIFFICULTIES Sunderland had in escaping League One put the achievement of the 1987/88 promotion winners into context. In the late 1980s the team bounced back at the first time of asking.

'To come back at the first attempt was an achievement. Because it's Sunderland you just think you should get promoted straight away but to actually do it was easier said than done.' So says Paul 'Jack' Lemon, who played in all but five of the 46 league games that year, scoring nine times in addition to a further three in the cups. 'Looking back at being part of a promotion team, it's just a feeling of pride. We shouldn't have gone down in the first place, but we did.'

It was the first time Sunderland had ever played in the third tier. Relegation had come as a result of a disastrous period under the management of Lawrie McMenemy. After McMenemy's infamous 'midnight flit', even the return of 1973 FA Cup-winning messiah Bob Stokoe had not been enough to prevent Sunderland going down. As in 2018 when Donald took over from Short the club had experienced a recent change at the top, Tom Cowie being replaced by Bob Murray.

Murray appointed Denis Smith as manager. Smith had done very well at York City but in the season before his appointment at Sunderland had endured a brush with relegation and seen his side knocked out of the FA Cup by non-league Caernarfon Town. A teak-tough centre-half as a player with Stoke, Smith did brilliantly at Sunderland. He produced a team that played attacking, stylish football and took the title by storm.

After starting with a 1-0 win at Brentford and then facing Middlesbrough in the League Cup, Lemon registered Sunderland's first-ever home goal in the third division, the opener in a 1-1 draw with Bristol Rovers. 'Nigel Martyn was in goal for Bristol Rovers,' remembers Paul of his strike against the future England keeper. 'It was at the Fulwell End, a cross-shot across the keeper, low into the corner. I hit it with my left foot. I seemed to score several of my better goals with my left foot.'

Always known as Jack rather than Paul – after the American film star Jack Lemmon – 'Jack' also scored in the next league match in an away win at Doncaster. He then played his part in a 4-1 home win over Mansfield that made Sunderland early leaders, but three draws followed by back-to-back defeats saw a slump to 12th. It was the lowest point in the club's history until 2019/20.

The last game of that five-match slide was a 2-0 home defeat to Chester. It marked the debut of teenage striker Marco Gabbiadini who Smith had plundered from his old club York. Gabbiadini hit the post against Chester before exploding on to the scene with braces in each of the next three games. The first of these at Fulham was the turning point of the season. 'We didn't get off to a great start after the first few games and we were mid-table at the end of September, but then we battered a few teams,' remembers Lemon. 'The improvement coincided with "Gabbers" coming in. As soon as he came in we played Fulham away and really kicked on from then.'

Fulham were joint top of the table as Gabbiadini goals in the first and last minutes secured a 2-0 victory at Craven Cottage. Something more than the confidence booster of victory occurred that night.

Gabbiadini had been signed to partner Keith Bertschin, but a broken jaw suffered by Bertschin caused a rethink. 'Eric Gates had been off form but got back into the team in my absence,' remembered Bertschin. 'He was such a great foil for Marco that even though I did well when I played I couldn't get a game a lot of the time.'

Gates hadn't even been on the bench at Fulham but was partnered with Gabbiadini for the first time the following Saturday as 'Marco Goalo' again scored twice as Aldershot were beaten. Seven days later as Gabbiadini bagged another brace, Gates got two of his own as Wigan were walloped 4-1.

The G-force became an attacking partnership since bettered only by Niall Quinn and Kevin Phillips. Gates and Gabbiadini were on the same wavelength. Former England international Gates became the sorcerer once he found his apprentice in Gabbiadini. Marco had the power and intelligence to run into space. Gates had the guile to guide the ball into his path. Once Gabbiadini was behind a defence there was no catching him. The G-force were more than Gates simply laying goals on a plate for his partner. Marco would tee up Eric as well. They would score 40 league goals between them in the promotion season, with Gates just two behind Gabbiadini's tally of 21.

'The combination of Gabbers and Gatesy really took off,' reminisces Lemon. 'Gatesy was going nowhere before Denis came but once we started playing through Eric, his vision and awareness with Gabbers was superb. Gabbers was a great signing.'

As Smith's team evolved, a problem at the other end was also in the process of being resolved. Like Gates, goalkeeper Iain Hesford had endured a difficult time during the dismal relegation of the previous term. He had been left out at the start of the season with on-loan stopper Steve Hardwick between the sticks. When Hardwick decided not to stay after six unbeaten league outings Hesford found himself required. 'I can't understand why Hesy got stick but he got a lot of it as I did as well,' recalls Lemon. 'When it happens you just get your head down and get on with it. Hesy being a goalkeeper, when we conceded goals he was the one that took a bit of stick.'

Hesford had conceded seven goals in two games against Gillingham in the play-offs as Sunderland were relegated. In the new season Gillingham had won their previous two home games 8-1 and 10-0, but Hesford came back into the team for an away game at the Gills and kept a clean sheet as a goalless draw was earned. Quickly rejuvenated – despite being beaten three times in his second game at eventual runners-up Brighton – Hesford went on to finish runner-up to Gates as Player of the Year, missing just one late-season game after coming back into the team. The son of Huddersfield's pre-war FA Cup Final goalkeeper Bob Hesford, Iain would pass away in 2014 at the age of just 54.

Hesford was helped by the dominance of two defenders Denis Smith had brought in at the beginning of the season. Both bought for bargain fees, centre-half John 'Monty' MacPhail and right-back John Kay would be the only two ever-presents. Kay became a cult hero on the terraces with his 'take no prisoners' approach, but it was 'Monty' MacPhail that 'Jack' Lemon feels had the biggest influence on the team.

'I think Monty was a great signing. He was rock solid at the heart of defence alongside Gary Bennett. Benno was brilliant but he had a mistake in him. Sometimes you'd see Benno flying down the left wing but sometimes you don't want your centre-halves doing that. Monty took no risks. It went in Row Z when it needed to. You never heard him much on the pitch. He didn't go around hammering people. He just did his job. Kaysie was a good signing but Kaysie was a right-back. If it's central, down the spine of the team and it works, I think they were the better signings, so for me Monty just gave that bit of edge to the team.'

MacPhail also added to the goal threat. Only the G-force scored more than the penalty-taking centre-half. No defender has ever matched MacPhail's record of 16 goals in a season. Eleven of those were penalties.

Following the 4-1 win over Wigan where each of the G-force scored twice, taking Sunderland to the top of the table, MacPhail scored both goals in the next game – one from the spot – as Blackpool were beaten at Bloomfield Road. Smith's former club York were on the end of a 4-2 scoreline, by which time a three-point gap had opened up to second-placed Walsall, with Northampton a further point behind.

In addition to the FA Cup and League Cup Sunderland also had to contest the Sherpa Van Trophy. A few days after beating York the Lads travelled to Scarborough for a first-ever appearance in this competition, in which Wembley was reached in 2019 and 2021, by which time it was named the Checkatrade, and later Papa John's, Trophy. Lemon netted two great goals from distance, one with each foot, to seal a 3-0 win. 'They were probably the best two goals I've scored,' recalls 'Jack', who explains, 'I know that Neil Warnock was in charge that day for Scarborough. In goal was Kevin Blackwell who went on to be his assistant at various clubs as well as managing teams like Leeds and Sheffield United himself.'

In the next round of the Sherpa Van Trophy Eric Gates destroyed Rotherham before being substituted at half-time. He hadn't scored but had created plenty as the interval arrived with Sunderland 6-1 up, Lemon amongst the scorers against a team managed by Norman Hunter. Another goal was added in the second half but after knocking out Crewe Sunderland came a cropper, embarrassingly going down 1-0 at home to Hartlepool – to a goal direct from a corner on the windiest of evenings.

In my view the extra eight games Sunderland played in the 2018/19 season in the same competition was a major factor in costing the club promotion. In 1987/88 eight cup games was the total for all competitions. Eliminated early on in the League Cup by Middlesbrough, interest in the FA Cup ended before Christmas in a second-round defeat at Scunthorpe.

Concentrating on the league was what the promotion campaign was about. The only league defeat in a 22-game league run from Marco's match at Fulham at the end of October until late February was a narrow Halloween loss at Notts County. The reaction to that was a strong one as three days later Southend United were slaughtered 7-0. Gates was a maker rather than a taker of goals as Rotherham had seven stuck past them later in the month, but on this occasion bagged four against the Shrimpers. After 21 years without scoring seven in a game, Sunderland did it twice in three weeks.

By this stage of the season Smith's Sunderland were playing some sublime football, a cut above what is associated with the third tier, then or now. Despite the despair felt when Sunderland had sunk into the third tier for the first time the previous summer, long before Christmas Roker Park was a happy place to be again. 'It was like any sort of work environment – if you're not happy, it's not a happy place to be. It doesn't matter where you work,' insists Lemon. 'Looking back I just think Denis brought a smile to everyone's face. I certainly enjoyed coming to training every day and it showed on the pitch because I kept my place a lot that season.

'The manager just put a big smile on people's faces. Denis liked a joke. Everyone had a bit of banter and took the mick out of each other. Denis wasn't one of the lads but he tried to get as close to us as possible, while certainly making clear to us who the manager was. It was just old school, even the training, but it was fun. We were well organised. We did a lot of shape work on the training ground but after that it was five-a-side, a bit of crossing, a bit of shooting.

'The squad that Denis inherited was a decent squad. You had young lads like "Owersy" [Gary Owers], Gordon [Armstrong] and myself. Mix that in with the experience that was there and we were far too good for most teams in that league. There are a lot of happy memories. We were poor the season before. I still say we should not have been relegated. That was poor. It's quite a nice feeling that we bounced back straight away. Denis came in as bad cop. Buzza [coach Viv Busby] was good cop. It all worked. Denis was very old school.

'Denis did promote team spirit. It was a happy place to work. We used to go out for a meal together on a Wednesday night. He encouraged us to go out together, obviously not going out and getting drunk, but just going out. The difference now is you can't do that, can you? The lads can't be seen to be going out because someone is going to play silly buggers with the public. Everybody's got video phones. I remember we used to go to a Chinese restaurant at Seaburn and nobody bothered us. People would say things like, "You were rubbish at the weekend – make sure you're better next week" or "Well done lads for Saturday." It was those sorts of comments. We never got personally slaughtered. Now it's like a superstar status. If I was a modern-day footballer I wouldn't go out. I just couldn't do it, which takes away a little bit of that team spirit. Whether they can get it in other ways, I'm not sure.'

Through the winter months as 1987 turned into 1988 the red and whites relentlessly continued their march. Away grounds were regularly packed to the rafters with the red and white army as Sunderland just kept winning. A home draw with Preston in the final match of the calendar year was the only league game in a sequence of nine games without a win bonus in the players' pay packets – Lemon getting the winners in the games either side of that draw.

By the time Brentford were beaten on 20 February a healthy six-point lead had been established – along with a game in hand and superior goal difference. Paul Lemon had played in every game but one but was sidelined for the Brentford game and the following week's trip to Bristol Rovers where the heaviest defeat of the season was suffered.

That game at Twerton Park was something of a disaster. Former Wolves stalwart Kenny Hibbitt suffered a career-ending injury in a challenge from Gordon Armstrong. Never a dirty player, Armstrong's challenge was entirely accidental but there was a lot of ill feeling afterwards. Rovers tore into Sunderland, inflicting a 4-0 thrashing with Ian Holloway getting the opening goal. Afterwards further disaster was narrowly averted when a ceiling light came crashing down and was left hanging inches above the water of a communal bath which some Sunderland players still occupied.

Paul Lemon has his own reason for remembering the occasion. 'I didn't play in that game. We played at Aldershot the following Tuesday night. Denis had told me to get on the train and come down because I was back in the team.' When Sunderland lost that game at Aldershot – to a winner from Sunderland old boy Steve Berry – back-to-back defeats meant Sunderland were knocked off the top of the table for the first time in over four months – albeit by one goal and still with a game in hand.

Given he missed the Bristol bashing Lemon was never in a side that lost by more than two goals that term, and says, 'I know we got beat that season but I can't remember anyone really giving us a beating. I don't remember ever walking off that season and feeling, "We've been turned over here." If somebody scored against us or we were one down at half-time I was always very confident we would come back and win the game. It was just the mentality we had.'

That mentality saw Fulham beaten next time out but when a run of three draws followed, Smith raided the transfer market to bring in midfielder Colin Pascoe from Swansea. 'Pasc, when he came in, was a good signing,' remembers Lemon. Wales international Pascoe was a talented footballer who made time for himself on the ball and gave the team new impetus in the closing weeks. It was another master stroke of Smith's to strengthen with new blood for the run-in, although his other new acquisition Dougie McGuire barely registered in the first team.

Pascoe was Swansea's top scorer that season as they won promotion from Division Four. He had scored in three of his four games for Sunderland when he went to Wembley with his new club.

In what was the centenary season of the Football League Sunderland had qualified for a special weekend tournament where teams from all divisions featured. Qualification had been based on league performance over a section of the campaign. In a 20 minutes each way game Sunderland faced fellow third-tier side Wigan, and after a goalless game lost 2-1 in a sudden-death penalty shoot-out where Pascoe's penalty was saved.

Goalkeeper Tim Carter had debuted at Wembley and made his league bow a week later against his home-town team Bristol City. When that game was lost as ex-Roker youth keeper Keith Waugh kept a clean sheet for the Robins, worries set in that Sunderland might slip up. The Lads had done so well, though, that they were still in a strong position at the top of the league.

A return to form came with a 4-0 midweek win at Mansfield whose ex-Newcastle keeper Eric Steele had conceded seven at Roker with Southend earlier in the season. Four days later Sunderland had the chance to secure promotion with victory at Port Vale. The problem was only Brighton had lost fewer home games than the Valiants.

'It was a horrible, scrappy game but I just knew we were going to score,' remembers Paul. 'They never bothered us that day and we didn't bother them much, but I just knew we were going to score with the Sunderland fans behind the goal. There must have been five or six thousand of us.' In fact, there were just 7,569 inside Vale Park that day, almost twice Vale's average. Paul might have been a little out on his estimation of the official gate but he was spot on in sensing a goal would come, as it did with just 11 minutes remaining. 'I was just hoping that the ball would fall to me to score but it was Gatesy who got it. That was us up.'

In an era of lower gates than modern-day football Sunderland's average of 17,424 was the only one in the division to reach five figures. It was also higher than eight clubs in the top division. The remaining home game against Northampton pulled in a crowd of 29,454, some 3,000 more than Newcastle's highest of the season for a Boxing Day top-flight meeting with Manchester United. The big gate saw Sunderland seal the third division championship with a 3-1 win, before a final-day party at Rotherham where 1973 cup winner Dave Watson was the guest of honour as two of his old clubs met.

Sunderland romped home 4-1, condemning the Millers to relegation via the play-offs. As in the promotions of 1964 and 1976, therefore (and as would happen again in 2007), the team Sunderland faced on the final day went down.

'I remember the Rotherham game because I scored an own goal!' remembers Paul. 'We had all the away fans down one side of the pitch, right behind the goal and then up to a certain point on the other side. The ball came over. I went to clear it with a header but I totally mistimed it and it hit my head and went over Iain Hesford's head and into the goal in front of the Sunderland fans. You can imagine the stick I got. It didn't take much.'

Regardless of the fact that he played regularly in a successful team, and but for the penalties of John MacPhail he would have been third top scorer behind the G-force, 'Jack' Lemon was often the butt of the crowd. Naturally a striker but utilised on the right of midfield, he was industrious and always had a goal in him, but still constantly had his critics.

'To play for Sunderland you have to have a thick skin. End of story,' he says, philosophically. 'If you've got someone playing wide right – say Luke O'Nien in recent years – and he's chipping in with ten to 12 goals, he's worth a few bob, so I totally get why Denis wanted to play me wide right so I could get in the box and get goals. It's just my natural game I learned when I played up top. I had to adapt my game, which I did, because if someone says you're playing for Sunderland you will adapt your game. You just do it.'

Only 24 when he left Sunderland in 1990 after over 100 games for the club, 'Jack' was forced to retire from full-time football just three years later after a cruciate ligament injury, although he extended his playing days in Norway, Ireland and non-league and maintains his relationship with the game into the 2020s as first-team scout for Scunthorpe United.

1989/90 DIVISION TWO PROMOTED

In this strangest of promotions, Sunderland finished sixth and then lost the play-off final against Swindon Town, only for the Robins to be denied promotion due to financial irregularities, with Sunderland going up in their place. Outstanding goalkeeper and record signing Tony Norman recalls Denis Smith's second promotion in three seasons.

SUNDERLAND WON promotion in 1990 even though they lost the play-off final after finishing sixth. Just two years earlier they had played in the third division. Following a season of mid-table consolidation, a challenge had been mounted. A good start meant that the Lads were briefly in an automatic promotion place, on goal difference, after a 3-2 home win over Bournemouth in early October. This would be the only time in the season the team would be in the top two, although they were third for a month around Christmas.

Leeds and Sheffield United eventually went up automatically, both on 85 points. Both games against Leeds had been lost without Sunderland scoring, but four points had been taken from the Blades, including a 3-1 win at Bramall Lane in a well-timed, best-of-season, four-game winning run that propelled the Lads from tenth to fifth just as the home straight was in sight.

As the end of the regular league season approached Sunderland knew they were guaranteed a play-off place with a game to spare after an away win at Port Vale, where promotion from the third division had also been secured two years before. So it was that on the final day there was no panic in losing 3-2 at home to Oldham. On the same day draws for Swindon and Blackburn guaranteed their play-off berths and took them both ahead of Sunderland on goal difference, all on 74 points. Newcastle could have dramatically gained an automatic promotion place had they won and either of the top two lost, but the Magpies' unbeaten nine-match run crashed as they were trounced 4-1at Middlesbrough where Bernie Slaven and Newcastle old boy Ian Baird each helped themselves to a couple. Had Sunderland even drawn with Oldham they would have finished fourth and met Swindon in the play-off semi-finals – but Swindon would have to wait for Wembley.

Goalkeeper Tony Norman was Sunderland's record signing at the time and takes up the story at the beginning of the end with those incredible play-offs. Sunderland convincingly triumphed 2-0 in the second leg at St James' with goals from each of the G-force of Gates and Gabbiadini, following a goalless first leg at Roker. That match ended in uproar.

'You couldn't have written it that we'd face Newcastle in the play-offs. It has to be one of the biggest derby games in the history of the fixture. We were fighting for promotion but also to get to Wembley so there was a double incentive. In the first leg at Roker Park the atmosphere was tense. Both clubs didn't want to give a thing away and I can't remember there being many chances at either end until we had a penalty in the last minute. We missed the penalty and [Tony chortles at the memory] in the aftermath Paul Hardyman gets sent off. Seconds beforehand we'd been thinking we had a chance of going to Newcastle with a slight advantage but now they were cock-a-hoop. As we walked off the pitch I shook hands with a couple of their lads and they were grinning from ear to ear. It was only half-time but they seemed to think they'd won it.

'When we got down the tunnel we turned left down the corridor to our dressing room as they turned right to theirs. All you could hear was them shouting, "Yessss!! Get in there!!!!" I was thinking, "They think they've won," and instantly the prickles were up on my neck and I was thinking, "Come on – keep that going." In my head – and I hadn't even got through our dressing-room door – I'm going, "The next game's going to be interesting." Once I did get into our dressing room the atmosphere was as flat as a pancake. Everybody was quiet. Denis and Buzza [manager and assistant Denis Smith and Viv Busby] were saying, "Come on lads, we've got another game." It was all quite subdued. I wasn't the biggest talker in the dressing room but I just looked at Denis and said, "We'll win you know – because they think they've got it. And they haven't! We'll go there and we'll win." He looked at me and said, "You honestly think that, don't you?" to which I replied, "I'm telling you!" As a dressing room we all went our separate ways that day but in the first training session back we were all ready for it. We knew what we had to do. We'd played Newcastle three times that season and they'd all been draws so they still hadn't beaten us. They thought they had the easy bit to come after drawing at our place.

'In the second leg they were the home team and they huffed and puffed, but when Mark McGhee hit the post I knew it wasn't going in. That's not an arrogant statement – I simply knew it wasn't on its way in. The only time I really had to make anything other than a routine save was once when the ball got knocked down in the penalty area and fell to one of their lads. I just spread myself and it hit me on the leg and went away. I didn't spend the 90 minutes flinging myself around. It was more a case of dealing with aerial things and reading situations. I remember the clock behind my goal that counted down the minutes but when I faced that way if I was retrieving the ball for a goal kick I wasn't clock-watching. In contrast, in another semi-final a couple of years later against Norwich at Hillsborough in the FA Cup they had a digital clock that counted down the minutes and I could have sworn that one had stopped!

'Against Newcastle, though, I just didn't feel that they could score. It was just a question of running the clock down. If they wanted to push on and leave Gatesey and Marco with a bit more space, the likelihood was that between the two of them they'd score another one. We had put ourselves in a position where I didn't feel they could unravel us.'

Eric Gates gave Sunderland an early lead, poaching a goal at the Gallowgate End after the athletic Gary Owers looped in a cross. As Tony says, he didn't have much to do. Sunderland's defence blocked almost all the home side had to offer so John Burridge was the busier keeper. He saved well from Owers and Gabbiadini before Marco applied the killer touch shortly before the end. Young Warren Hawke – in for the suspended Hardyman with Reuben Agboola dropping into the left-back berth – slid the ball to Marco. It was at this point that the G-force blew away the Magpies.

The partnership between Gates and Gabbiadini had been destroying teams for three years. This would be the 105th goal the pair had plundered in those three seasons, and the last as the G-force as Gates would leave after the play-off final. Marco and Eric knew each other's games inside out. As so often before, Gabbiadini played the ball in to his partner and began running into space the moment he'd played it. With Jim Baxter-like pinpoint accuracy and weight of pass Gates delivered the return into his mate's path and it was goodnight Newcastle, as in front of the red and white hordes squeezed in behind the Leazes End goal one of the most important derbies of all time was settled.

It was too much to bear for the idiotic element of the home crowd – although most sensible United supporters were simply devastated and remained in their places, or slunk home early. However, hordes came on to the pitch in an attempt to get the game abandoned as they had done in 1974 when losing an FA Cup tie at home to Nottingham Forest, only to win the replay and go on to Wembley. There was to be no Wembley for the black and whites this time thanks to Spennymoor referee George Courtney, who was about to officiate at Italia 90 having refereed at the previous FIFA World Cup finals, as well as taking a European final in 1989.

'I can never forget when the crowd came on,' remembers Norman. 'It was a handful at first before they came on in droves. George

Courtney was the ref and he pointed towards the dressing rooms and off the lads went. I picked up my spare gloves out of the back of my net and I actually walked off. What a berk I was! The crowd were running past me. I meandered off and all the players congregated in the tunnel area with George Courtney stood beside us. We were itching to finish the game but the Newcastle lads looked flattened. George Courtney said, "Gentlemen. I will say one thing now to you all. We will be finishing this game tonight and I don't care if we have to restart it at midnight." Our lads were going, "Get in!" Not loudly but you could see we were all thinking, "We'll have a bit of this." At the same time you could physically see shoulders drop amongst the black and white lads. When both teams went back on to the playing surface you just knew it was a matter of running the clock down. The few minutes eased past and we knew George wasn't going to add six minutes of injury time on or anything stupid. The game finished and we were over the moon, while the Newcastle lads were resigned to their fate.'

Fate would also play a part in the final. Swindon Town were to be the opponents after beating Blackburn home and away in their own semi-final. The season had started with an away win over the Robins, while the sides had shared four goals at Roker in December. Ahead of the final, rumours were circling that Swindon were going to be in trouble because of financial irregularities.

The People newspaper – inspired by Sunderland-supporting journalist Bill Bradshaw – had been investigating matters at Swindon for some time. In essence, Swindon were alleged to have made in the region of 35 illegal payments to players. They were also alleged to have bet on themselves to win the 1987 Division Three title – apparently as an 'insurance policy' to cover bonuses that would have to be paid if they were successful (this was in contravention of FA rules) – and had also apparently bet on themselves to lose an FA Cup tie, ironically with Newcastle, which they did to the tune of 5-0 in 1988.

Following a third *People* exposé into matters at the club in January of 1990, the following month the Inland Revenue revealed there was to be an investigation into Swindon's affairs and this was scheduled for the end of the season. Initially pencilled in for 4 May before the play-offs this was postponed on legal advice until June, but by this time Swindon chairman Brian Hillier and secretary Vince Farrar had been arrested, as had manager Lou Macari. Former Manchester United player Macari was subsequently cleared but Hillier and Farrar were found guilty.

Although Swindon beat Sunderland 1-0 in the play-off final, as their fans celebrated and Sunderland's departed Wembley with the all-too-often-experienced disappointment at the national stadium, in due course Swindon were punished by being denied promotion with losing finalists Sunderland promoted in their place. Initially, Swindon were actually demoted to the third tier, although this was later lifted and their punishment was to simply miss promotion. Perhaps had Sunderland beaten them at Wembley they would have been relegated?

While some supporters clung on to the hope that Sunderland might possibly go up if Swindon were found guilty and punished, Tony Norman insists this was not something that had been considered amongst the squad. 'We had no inkling at all. As inklings go. If an inkling is ten per cent of a chance it was 100th of an inkling. If someone had mentioned something in passing it would have been dismissed out of hand as nothing more than wishful thinking. We went into the game with not even an idea of that happening. We got beat and obviously we were disappointed but afterwards the story started appearing in the media saying there was a chance that Swindon were going to be stopped from getting promoted. The next thing is you are waiting for news and everybody jumped on the bandwagon. Newcastle appealed because they had finished third.'

As a past (and future) president of the Football League, Newcastle United's chairman Gordon McKeag, a solicitor, was well placed to make a strong case for his club. Having been relegated narrowly on goal difference as the highest-placed relegated club, Sheffield Wednesday also protested that if Swindon were being denied promotion they should retain their place in the top flight. The Owls' case was spearheaded by their chairman Dave (later Sir Dave) Richards, a future chairman of the Premier League, again a stern advocate.

Beavering away diligently behind the scenes, however, it was Sunderland's young chairman Bob Murray who ensured Sunderland's cause would hold sway, and if anyone was to benefit from Swindon's demise it would be Sunderland, who had reached the play-off final. The news that it was Sunderland to be promoted came as a surprise to goalkeeper Norman. 'I can remember being in the back garden when it came on the radio that we were going up. Then I started thinking, "What if Newcastle win an appeal?" It was only when it was written in tablets of stone and Sunderland were confirmed as promoted that you could really believe it.'

Given the counterclaims of Newcastle United and Sheffield Wednesday, the decision to promote Sunderland would have surely been so much harder to arrive at had Sunderland lost the play-off final heavily rather than 1-0. This could so easily have been the case but for Tony playing a blinder on an afternoon when Sunderland were comprehensively outplayed. Making a series of great saves, particularly from Steve White, Duncan Shearer and one where, not unusually, he denied Tom Jones with his feet after looking beaten, Norman was only conquered by a shot that took a huge deflection.

'It's like watching a slow-motion film in my head,' says Tony of the only goal from the play-off final. 'I can remember him [Alan McLoughlin] picking it up. I can see him striking it right-footed and in all honesty, I'm going to my right. I can see how high it's going to get to, it's about a foot off the floor, it's going to be comfortable and I know it's a catch not a parry. In slow-motion terms I knew that instantly but then Benno [Gary Bennett] poked out his foot and it hit him but I'd gone – I was past the stage of my weight still being on my feet. My body's weight was moving to where the ball would have been. There was no getting back and after it hit Benno I could see it spinning – I could just about hear it spinning – and I just knew it was going in. When he hit the ball it was a save, but after it hit Benno I was powerless. I still look back and say we got beat 1-0 because of a deflection. That's what galls me. That's the way I've always looked at it, but it's a fair point – what would have happened if we'd got drubbed that day?'

Indeed, had the Wembley score been four or five nil, which it could quite easily have been, would the suits around the deciding table have been able to conclude that it should be Sunderland who were promoted?

Manager Denis Smith's achievement in taking over at Sunderland following their first-ever relegation to the third division and steering the club into the top flight within three seasons should never be underestimated. The understanding of the time was that Denis Smith was bad cop and Buzza [assistant Viv Busby] was good cop with the squad, as suggested by 'Jack' Lemon who talked about their earlier promotion success. Asking Tony if this is too simplistic a way of looking at things elicits an emphatic single-word reply: 'Yes!' He elaborates: 'Denis was brilliant. When I signed for Sunderland I came up and stayed the first night with the family in the County Hotel in Durham. Denis and his wife came in that evening, sat with us that night to make sure we were alright and stressed that if there was anything he or his wife Kate could do, not to hesitate to let them know. If there was stick to dish out after a game, Denis, as manager, would do it. He'd tell people to their face. There's nothing wrong with that. You take it, say, "Fair point" and get on with it. You could never look at Denis and say he was simply "bad cop" because he would fight hammer and tongs for his players, and you knew it. Yes, he might tell you you were rubbish today and he might leave you out, but he would always fight your corner and as a manager that's what you need. He could be a bad cop but as a person and a manager you knew he'd stick up for you. Viv was Viv and as a pair they were superb working together.

'Denis would never want to just lump it in and fight for it. You'd never really hear those sorts of words. He had Benno at centre-half and Benno had a bit of finesse about him. Benno would come out and play. As a goalkeeper with Benno at centre-half, I'd look at him and think, "Where's he going now?" We'd be winning 1-0 with two minutes to go and Benno would decide to join in with the front two! I roomed with him for six and a half years. Some of the things he'd do, you'd just laugh – especially as he could be so serious. He was great. The way I saw any game is I was looking at my back four and then ahead of them I'd see the midfield. The way I saw the game was that it was my back four and if someone wasn't where I wanted them to be I'd be thinking, "Whoa, where are you going?"'

During the same season one of the places Benno infamously ended up was in the Clock Stand paddock with Coventry's David Speedie in a League Cup quarter-final when both were sent off. Tony didn't have to worry about Benno going AWOL that night as Tim Carter kept goal in the cup ties having started the run when playing during Tony's injury absence. Injury cost Norman his place for much of the first half of the promotion season. 'I broke my wrist with about 20 minutes to go at West Brom. It came from a back pass which ended up being a 50–50 between myself and the forward. I led with my arms and obviously the lad led with his foot and my wrist was broken. There were no subs in those days – keeper-wise – so we decided I'd just stop on. I was supposed to be travelling to join up with the Welsh squad after the game but Steve Smelt, who was the physio, said, "You can't report like this" and phoned the Welsh FA. I was strapped up and when the strapping came off we took one look at it and went for an X-ray. It was broken. I was out two or three months and missed about 17 games.

'I played at a time when you didn't jump from club to club to club. You signed for a club and until you were told it was time to leave, in my head it was all about staying at your club. I'd been at Hull for nine and a half years and then on Boxing Day in 1988 after the game, I got called into the office and told somebody has come in for you and you can go. I asked which club it was and when I was told it was Sunderland I had to think, "Crikey, how far is that away?" Within days my life had changed and my next game was on New Year's Eve at Roker Park against Portsmouth. If someone had said to me at the point that I left Hull that I'd go on to play in the top division, go to Wembley twice with one of them being an FA Cup final you'd think, "Flipping heck, I'll take that." I can't say anything but good things of the move. As a footballing decision it was brilliant, especially with playing at Wembley twice. It taught me a lot about camaraderie and how things work. I learned a lot about people. The experience of it was terrific.'

Sunderland were good for Tony Norman but unquestionably Tony was also good for Sunderland. Carrying on in the fine tradition of the club's goalkeepers, he was an outstanding custodian who rarely made an error. There have been many heroes of many promotions but had Sunderland been hammered in the 1990 play-off final, the strangest of promotions that was settled around a table might never have been confirmed. Arguably, Tony Norman could be the greatest promotion hero of them all.

1995/96 DIVISION ONE CHAMPIONS

Top scorer Craig Russell talks us through Peter Reid's first full season in charge.

CRAIG RUSSELL top-scored in 1995/96 as promotion to the top flight was won for the first time since the creation of what was then called the FA Carling Premiership. It was the season when the 'Cheer Up Peter Reid' chant became the soundtrack in what was Reidy's first full campaign, as Sunderland entered an era where Reid brought success and excitement in a period of change. The league title would be the final silverware brought to Roker Park in the penultimate season at the ground. With the Premiership having its own cup, the grand old Football League championship trophy returned to Wearside for the first time since 1936, when Raich Carter, Bobby Gurney and co secured the club's sixth top-flight title. At that point no team had been champions of England more than Sunderland, but sadly, in the post-war era it is promotions rather than top-flight titles that have had to sustain the generations – those and the FA Cup on 5 May 1973.

Born on 4 February 1974, Russell always claims he was conceived as part of the cup-winning celebrations. Coming from a Sunderland-supporting family, going on to create his own part of SAFC history is something Russ reflects on still with some astonishment. 'It was almost surreal. When you've been a fan and you come through to be part of a team that's won the league. It's the kind of moment where you think, "Is this really happening?" You cannot believe it. My family were almost in a state of shock about everything that was going on. To have won the league and for their son or brother being the top goalscorer was a lot to take in.'

When Roker Park closed a year after Russell's promotion-winning season, at the farewell match against Liverpool Craig broke away from the warm-up to rush and shake the hand of Gary Rowell, as former stars paraded around the pitch. Like Rowell, Russell was still a fan and remains one. In 2021 he is still at the club as a masseur, a role he has carried out since 2009, in addition to his 174 appearances as a player.

It was Russell who lit the blue touchpaper when Reid arrived. Given seven games to keep Sunderland up in 1995 after the departure of Mick Buxton, like all managers in such a situation, Reid needed to get off to a positive start. With 19 minutes left of his first game at home to Sheffield United and the game goalless, Reid brought Russell off the bench. 'It was such a big surprise when Reidy walked in the door,' remembers Russ. 'It came from nowhere. Mick Buxton had taken the team as far as he could and change was needed. Luckily enough I was the one to get Reidy off to a perfect start. I just remember coming on as a sub and I'm almost sure one of their lads got sent off. I was clean through and he brought me down. Steve Agnew played a ball over the top late on. I managed to get away from the defender and just smashed it as hard as I could. Luckily for me and the club at that time, it just trickled over the line after goalkeeper Alan Kelly managed to take the pace off it without being able to stop the shot.'

David Tuttle was the Blade banished for felling Russell four minutes after he had replaced Brett Angell against Dave Bassett's side. Sunderland went on to finish eight points clear of the drop.

Reid renewed his relationship with his old Everton midfield partner Paul Bracewell, who returned in the summer for a third spell at the club he had left for Newcastle after captaining the Wearsiders in the 1992 FA Cup Final. Brought in as player-assistant manager, Brace would add nous and composure to the team as Craig explains. 'I'd watched Brace as a supporter but it was when I was playing alongside him that I appreciated how good he was as a player, especially after the injuries he'd had.'

Bracewell was the only 'new' face in the side on the opening day of the season when a home defeat to Leicester City indicated that perhaps another year of struggle was in store. That feeling was furthered when Sunderland found themselves 19th after five games. Within that spell Reid had read a riot act stronger than anything seen on the following season's *Premier Passions*. This came at half-time of a League Cup second-leg tie when Sunderland trailed 2-0 at home to bottom-tier Preston (who would win their league that season too). Stung by the gaffer's rage the Lads came back to win 3-2, but it was after Russell's first goal of the season that Sunderland started to get into the groove.

Speaking to Craig, I couldn't remember his goal that provided a turning-point 1-0 win against Southend in September – I'd just looked it up – but it is a strike that has stayed in Russell's memory. 'I don't want to blow my own trumpet but it was a canny goal, that one. I intercepted a wayward pass from a Southend player. I was just over the halfway line and I managed to take a big touch, burst past a couple of defenders and shot from the inside-left area of the box beyond the goalkeeper and into the bottom corner. My abiding memory of that one was that Mickey Gray had had a bit of a fallout with Reidy and he'd got subbed, and Bally had got sent off that day as well for a robust challenge on the former Liverpool player Mike Marsh. Southend were a bit of a bogey team at Roker Park in that era but we managed to cling on.'

Victory over the Shrimpers set Sunderland off on an 11-match unbeaten league run that took them up to fourth. Including the Southend game Russell only started six of these fixtures, scoring in two of them. Often used off the bench, but sometimes left on it, Craig was fighting hard for a place in the team. When he did get an opportunity he regularly found himself out wide instead of in his preferred role of through the middle.

After seeing the unbeaten run come to an end at Stoke, 1-0 wins over West Brom and Palace – without Russell featuring – took

Sunderland into a top-of-the-table clash at home to Mick McCarthy's Millwall.

Although Russell was in and out of the team at this point, generally Reid was fielding a settled XI. Bracewell had been ever present until limping out of the action a couple of games earlier at his first club Stoke. Alec Chamberlain and Polish right-back Dariusz Kubicki were ever present – 'Dariusz was just Mr Consistent. Seven out of ten guaranteed nearly every week,' recalls Russell. Alongside them Martin Scott, Andy Melville, Kevin Ball, Mickey Gray, Dicky Ord and Phil 'Tippy' Gray were regulars, while David 'Ned' Kelly had been brought in from Wolves. Kelly effectively became Sunderland's first £1m player when a £100,000 add-on to his £900,000 transfer fee was included as promotion was secured, but he injured himself against Palace and subsequently only made another couple of appearances that season.

With much of the club's financial resources going towards plans for a new stadium, losing the player so much money had been invested in was a blow. An overdraft in excess of £2m was revealed in late November, just a couple of weeks after chairman Murray declared, 'An historic milestone for Sunderland Football Club' as the Tyne and Wear Development Corporation gave planning permission for a new stadium at Wearmouth Colliery.

With Kelly unavailable there was a place up for grabs against Millwall. 'There was a bit of a back story to the Millwall game,' reveals Russell. 'David Kelly, who we had not long signed, had got injured and was going to be out for a long spell. We were playing Barnsley reserves away and, in those days, if you weren't in the first team you played in the reserves. Peter Reid came to me and John Mullin and said, "You're both going to play a half. It's up to you who plays the first half and who plays the second. It's up to you to take your chance because one of you will be playing on Saturday." John Mullin wanted to play the first half so when I came on I thought, "This is my chance," and I just kept running and working and I might have scored, I can't remember.' In fact, Russ scored just a minute after coming on at Oakwell and remembers, 'Pop Robson was the manager and afterwards he said, "Well done. After that I think it's going to be you on the Saturday," but you never knew with

Reidy. Anyway, I got the nod. It was a top-of-the-table clash against Millwall and on the day everything just went right. Smithy was on fire, creating things, and Phil Gray was on top form but all the chances fell to me.'

Russell scored four times as Millwall were lashed 6-0 and picks out his favourite as 'The first one. Millwall had a corner which I was back for. I got a block on a pass which fell to Smithy. I started a run from well inside my own half and Smithy being Smithy, knowing me and where I wanted the ball, slotted it perfectly through. I managed to get on the end of it at full pace, got a good connection on it and shot across Kasey Keller and into the bottom corner. That put us 2-0 up going into half-time. Smithy used to pick me out all the time when we were playing together.'

Craig's understanding with Martin Smith was reminiscent of the link-up between Kevin Arnott and Gary Rowell almost two decades earlier, but whereas 'Ossie' Arnott and Rowell had plenty of opportunities to show what they could do, Russ remembers, 'Unfortunately, we didn't get the chance to play together too often with me as a striker and Smithy as a wide man. When we first got in the team together it was when Mick Buxton was manager and a lot of the time I was wide and Smithy was wide.'

Craig's choice of his four goals as the first was the 12th goal he'd scored at the Fulwell End, with his second-half hat-trick at the Roker End being his first goals at that end of the ground. Having joined the select band of players to have scored four goals in a game for Sunderland must be something that gave Craig added belief in himself: 'I always felt with Reidy I was half a bad game from being left out, so after scoring the four goals I thought he can't just suddenly leave me out. People tend to forget I was still only 21 and I was the main striker for Sunderland AFC. I was only 23 when I left. I was still a baby almost in the terms of nowadays. I think scoring the four goals made me think I was going to get another six, seven, maybe eight games in the team, surely.'

Russell's four-goal haul came on only the second time he'd played through the middle all season. He had scored against Barnsley on the previous occasion. Peter Reid acknowledged, 'To be fair to Craig

Russell, I've played him out of position and he's done a good job for me. He's been itching to play up front.'

Following the Lion-taming act against Millwall, Russ remained as a striker for virtually all of the rest of the season, but the next few games saw Sunderland struggle to score. Only one of the next nine league games was won. On that occasion a 1-0 win over Grimsby provided the only goal scored in six league games and resulted in scorer Richard Ord setting off in a celebration of Olympic sprint-standard speed.

During this barren run Russell did score in a thrilling 2-2 cup draw with Manchester United at Old Trafford. Earlier in the season the Lads had played some excellent football without reward in the League Cup against Liverpool. At Anfield Mickey Gray's only penalty before his ill-fated one at Wembley against Charlton in the 1998 play-off final had also been saved. A few days after the replay with United was lost 2-1 Reid sprang a surprise by dropping consistent goalkeeper Alec Chamberlain, who had kept nine clean sheets in 23 league games. In his place came an unknown teenager on loan from Blackburn Rovers. 'Reidy blamed Alec for Cantona's equaliser at Man United,' says Craig. 'Once Reidy makes his mind up that's it – it's really hard to change it. All of a sudden, in walks Shay. Everybody was like, "Who is this guy?" I think it was Leicester away and Reidy just chucked him in. Shay kept a clean sheet that day and went from strength to strength. He was unbelievable in that spell of games.'

Indeed, Given was incredible before an Easter injury at Barnsley brought Chamberlain back for the run-in, during which Chamberlain started with five successive clean sheets, only being beaten in the last game of the season, by which time the title had been secured. Given's elasticity, agility and bravery were exceptional. He was called up for the first of 134 Republic of Ireland caps while on loan to Sunderland, where he conceded goals in only five of his 17 appearances.

At one point Given kept five consecutive clean sheets. The fifth of these came in a crunch game at home to Derby, who would finish as runners-up behind Sunderland. The Rams were seven points ahead of the Lads, who had two games in hand. Under Jim Smith

Derby were unbeaten in 20 games stretching back over four months, but Sunderland were full of belief. 'We went into it feeling really confident. The lads at the back were doing a great job, Shay Given was being unreal and we just thought, "We're not getting beat here." We knew if we won it was a real statement because Derby were flying as well. I remember it being a really electric atmosphere right from arriving at Roker Park. You go into some games thinking, "We're not losing today" and that was one of those. There was no fear. I scored early on and then Aggers [Steve Agnew] made it 2-0 before half-time when we felt we had the game where we wanted it.'

Russell scored his second of the game after the break to wrap up a 3-0 win against Marco Gabbiadini's Derby. Craig had scored in the previous game as Grimsby were beaten 4-0 at Blundell Park just as the 'Cheer Up Peter Reid' chant was getting going. By this time Sunderland had promotion written all over them. It wasn't just the players who had belief, the fans did too. The Derby game was the fifth in a sequence of nine successive wins that began with a Russell winner against Ipswich.

The last of those victories looked like being a defeat as Sunderland trailed at home to Huddersfield with nine minutes left. With former Roker keeper Tony Norman excelling for the Terriers most people would have been happy with a point, but 17-year-old substitute Michael Bridges burst forth with two goals to seal a 3-2 victory. Nine successive wins equalled the club record in all competitions and was the best in the league alone since the Team of All Talents won their first league title in 1891/92. Bridges was the youngest of a group of young players Peter Reid blended with his more experienced men. Unfortunate to later be at the club when Kevin Phillips and Niall Quinn blocked his path, Bridges moved to Leeds for £5m and would have surely played for England but for suffering badly from injuries.

Although the winning run was halted in the tenth game as Russell scored in a 3-3 draw at Watford, the team remained unbeaten for a total of 18 league matches, only being defeated on the final day of the season at Tranmere, by which time promotion had been secured. Appropriately for a title win based on a strong defence, a sequence of four goalless draws either side of a 3-0 win over Birmingham – where Russell registered the final goal of the campaign – took Sunderland over the line and into the Premiership.

In the final analysis it was the skipper of the 2005 promotion winners who scored the goal that mathematically wrapped up promotion in 1996. Gary Breen got Birmingham's equaliser against Derby that secured Sunderland's elevation 24 hours before Sunderland took a point from a home game with Stoke. As people waited for the news from Derby, Peter Reid was at Feethams watching Darlington take on Bury who he had played for the previous season.

The season had been based on a tight defence. The 33 goals conceded in 46 games was 15 fewer than anyone else. From Russell's position in the team as the 'Jarrow Arrow' spearheading the side, was it a case of defending from the front or did Reid require Russell to retain his energy for a ball over the top? 'Reidy wanted me to stretch the game. If somebody's willing to run that takes the pressure off. You might run and never get the ball but it takes you right up the field and the game away from your goal. A big part of the team thinking was if we've got a bit of pace up there we can use it to get up the field. If we get a throw-in or whatever it's getting us into the opposition's half.'

Going down in history as the top scorer in a promotion-winning season is rightly a source of pride. 'It's something no one can ever take away from me. I'm an avid reader of fanzine stuff and it makes me laugh sometimes when people say things like Sunderland hardly scored that year and the top scorer to win the championship only had 13 goals. What they don't realise is that as top scorer I didn't actually play that much. If they count the number of minutes I spent on the pitch it would look a bit different. Reidy used to take me off almost every week. I only started 35 games and I read things like that and think, "Hold on a minute – I was only 21 years old and I didn't play that much really,"' he laughs.

Russ is right. He played under three-quarters of the available time, a total of 2,955 of the available 4,140 minutes, many of those out wide where he spent the bulk of his 894 minutes prior to his four-goal haul against Millwall. Nine of Craig's goals came in the 16 occasions he got the full 90 minutes, with a tenth in a match where he was subbed with two minutes to go.

Phil Gray's eight goals made him second-top scorer and the only other man to notch more than five, so did Craig feel under pressure to score? 'I didn't look at it like that. I just went out to do my best,' he says. 'We worked as a team and my first thought was always to work as hard as I possibly could and that would help everybody. I didn't really think, "I've got to score today", I just felt I've got to make an impression today.'

Craig certainly did make an impression and in being top scorer in a promotion season with 13 goals, he is in good company. Both Pop Robson exactly 20 years before and David Connolly ten years later topped the charts with the same number. Who says 13 is unlucky?

1998/99 DIVISION ONE CHAMPIONS

*Winger Allan 'Magic' Johnston remembers a
phenomenal season in which Peter Reid's red
and whites set a national-record 105 points and
reached the League Cup semi-final.*

JUST AS the first-ever promotion side of 1963/64 are revered, the same goes for the 105-point team of 1998/99. Already over two decades in the past, as further years go by supporters will become more and more misty-eyed at the memories of a team who played with enormous flair and set so many records. Partnerships make teams and while, usually, celebrated duos are forwards, the class of 1998/99 had partnerships running throughout the side.

Winger Allan Johnston's left-flank link-up with Michael Gray was a key part of the magic formula that manager Peter Reid had conjured up. Both players made their international debuts that season, Johnston for Scotland against Estonia in October (the first of six caps won that season, scoring in the last two of them) and Gray for England away to Hungary in April. That game also saw Kevin Phillips's international debut as for the first time since 1926 (Albert McInroy and Warney Cresswell) Sunderland had two players in the same England line-up.

Sometimes partnerships have to be worked on and developed. At other times they seem made in heaven and come naturally. 'It was one of those ones that just clicked to be honest,' says Allan 'Magic' Johnston of his combination with Gray. 'Especially with me being right-footed playing on the left. It suited me, especially with Mickey's pace and his fitness going up and down the line. It suited me having someone on the overlap because it allowed me to come inside and give him the ball – sometimes,' he laughs. 'It went through the whole team. There were partnerships all over the park. The central defenders [Andy Melville and Paul Butler] were good together, and then in midfield you had Bally [Kevin Ball] who was the sitter with someone else who was more attack-minded such as Lee Clark or Alex Rae, and then there were Chris [Makin] and Nick [Summerbee] on the right.

'They were different to what we were on the other side. Nicky's crosses were just incredible. Obviously we scored so many goals and when you look back so many of them came from crosses and set pieces – especially when you've got targets like Niall Quinn and Kevin Phillips in the box. It was hard to miss them to be honest. You've got to remember as well that Kev was small but he was so aggressive in the air. Even in games when you were struggling to make a breakthrough he'd come up with a moment of magic. They could always produce something, even if it was just a half chance.

'It's easy to forget how many important players were injured that season and that just shows you the quality of the squad that we had that people could come in and step up to the plate.' Even injuries to the front two of Super Kevin Phillips and Niall Quinn couldn't derail the promotion charge, as young Mickey Bridges and Danny Dichio came in and notched 20 league goals between them. After breaking Brian Clough's post-war seasonal scoring record the previous year, Phillips missed four months of the campaign after being injured in a League Cup win over Chester. Returning with a wonder-goal volley at QPR, Superkev still managed an incredible 23 goals in 26 league appearances. Goodness knows how many he'd have bagged if he had been fit all season.

Niall Quinn also missed five early fixtures. Returning to the side as a sub in a home game with Oxford, when Superkev was still missing, Sunderland's strength in depth was indicated by a

7-0 scoreline. Stand-ins Mickey Bridges and Danny Dichio helped themselves to a brace each against the U's.

Sunderland swept all before them. No team at any club had ever registered as many points. Sunderland had never won more league games than the 31 victories in this campaign, nor lost as few as the meagre three from 46 suffered. From the start of the season they went a record 23 games unbeaten in all competitions, while a record 30 clean sheets were recorded.

Being part of such a joyful team was obviously tremendous, with Allan explaining that the seeds of success were sown immediately after the disappointment of losing the previous season's play-off final on penalties after a 4-4 Wembley draw with Charlton. 'I think it probably started the year before. That season didn't start that well but following our relegation we started to climb the table and went on a fantastic run and then obviously we got beat in the play-offs. At the end when you heard Niall speaking, I think that gave inspiration to everybody and instilled the belief that in the next year we were going to go on and win the league. That came through perhaps because of what happened at Wembley. Sometimes when things don't go as planned then everybody rallies round and you get together. There was a real team spirit about the squad. We'd been on a really good run and after listening to Quinny we were all fired up.'

Phillips scored in each of the opening three games. An opening-day penalty defeated QPR in front of over 40,000 at the Stadium of Light before a draw at Swindon. Nine goals were then rattled in in the next two home games. This took the Lads to the top of the table, where they would spend almost the whole season. The first of seven goals scored by Johnston came in the last of that opening quartet, a 4-1 win over Watford, but it is a game from the end of the previous campaign that Johnno recalls vividly: 'I think the one I remember the most was the season before in the play-off semi-finals, just because of the atmosphere against Sheffield United. It was absolutely unbelievable, probably the best I ever played in,' says the man who played in two Old Firm derbies for Rangers but sadly never a Wear–Tyne derby.

Even without the brilliant first-choice front two Sunderland were quickly cruising. 'I remember the atmosphere which was incredible,' says Johnston. 'Every week the place was packed and the atmosphere was unbelievable with everyone getting right behind the team. It was just a really positive time to be at the club. Moving to the Stadium of Light had been a big factor as well.'

Johnston had written his name into the record books as the scorer of the last-ever league goal at Roker Park, and in the first two seasons at the new ground proceeded to thrill supporters with his ability to drop his shoulder and leave his marker with twisted blood. Whether he went inside or outside the full-back, whether he crossed for the front men, slid a ball to the overlapping Gray or jinked inside and curled a shot to the far top corner, Johnston was absolutely top drawer.

That wasn't just true of Johnno but applied to the whole team. Usually, even successful sides have a blip at some point in the season. The class of '98/99 saw their worst league run be three successive draws, while on each of the three occasions they lost they immediately bounced back with a victory. Forwards, of course, get the headlines but the biggest difference between the 105-point season and the previous year, when 90 points hadn't been sufficient for promotion, was in defence.

Debuting on the opening day were goalkeeper Thomas Sørensen and centre-back Paul Butler, both of whom went on to become full internationals. In attack five more goals were scored than the season before but the influence of Sørensen and Butler resulted in the number conceded being almost halved – just 28 goals were let in compared with 50 in the previous year. 'They were two top players. Thomas came in and straight away you could tell he was going to have a big future in the game. Even in training he was one of those boys who hated losing a goal. The calibre of players Peter Reid signed was excellent and "Butts" was another diamond. Centre-halves don't get a lot of attention sometimes but he was a big, solid centre-half. He was aggressive and scored a few goals as well. Obviously the defensive record was there for everybody to see.'

Alongside the triumphal procession of the promotion season, like the team of '64, the '98/99 team also went on a cup run, in their case reaching the semi-final of the League Cup, then sponsored by Worthington. Nine games were played in the competition, York and Chester being beaten in both legs of the two-legged early rounds that resulted in Phillips being lost to injury. Extra time was required to see off Grimsby at home, before Everton were beaten in a penalty shoot-out at Goodison on a night where Mickey Bridges scored sublimely. As in the 1973 FA Cup triumph Luton were beaten at home in the quarter-final, but Sunderland came a cropper against Martin O'Neill's Leicester City in the semi. Beaten 2-1 at home in the first leg to two clinical Tony Cottee finishes, Sunderland travelled to Filbert Street and looked like overturning the deficit. A Niall Quinn goal brought the aggregate level but on the night Leicester received news that they would receive planning permission for their own new stadium, the half-time introduction of Robbie Savage, combined with what was felt to be some weak refereeing by David Elleray, saw Leicester disrupt Sunderland's flow and go through with Cottee's third goal of the tie.

While it would have been nice to go to Wembley, the old twin towers held disappointing recent memories and Sunderland certainly didn't want to return there in the play-offs. Automatic promotion was rightly the aim and just three days after going out of the League Cup goals from Johnston and Quinn earned three hard-won points at home to Wolves. The fact a bigger crowd saw that game than the home leg of the semi-final with Leicester illustrated that the fans also saw promotion as the priority.

That tight defence produced three consecutive clean sheets going into a visit to Bradford City who would be runners-up. At the time the Bantams were third but with a game in hand on Ipswich who they could climb above into the second promotion place if they could beat the Lads.

In a game as hard-fought as might be expected given the stakes, Quinn scored the only goal of the game from a Johnston corner. Ever the man for the big occasion, Niall took his heroics a stage further by going in goal after Sørensen had to go off injured. Donning the blue keeper's top, at one point Niall came flying off his line Superman-style. Unorthodox he may have been but the Mighty Quinn kept his clean sheet intact. This was an occasion when the character of the team shone through. Mostly they were simply too good for the rest of the division and had the professionalism to ensure that consistency was never lacking.

With Peter Reid and Bobby Saxton in charge that was never likely. Saxton was loved by the players and deserves much of the credit for Sunderland's success during this period, but the team Reid had assembled was made up of characters as Johnston outlines. 'Guys like Kevin Ball – he's a leader, isn't he? He's one of those guys who leads from the front and we had a lot of those guys in the team, people like Lee Clark, Alex Rae, Andy Melville, Paul Butler and so on, so there was a lot of experience and a lot of real winners. The main thing with that team was that everyone knew their jobs. They knew exactly how they were going to play and it probably suited the players we had.'

After the win at Bradford, Sunderland had a 12-point lead over second-placed Ipswich and 15 points on Bradford who retained a game in hand as Sunderland had ten fixtures to play. It was only ever a question of the gap getting wider, not narrower. A draw at Crystal Palace saw the only points dropped from the next five games as Sunderland headed to Bury in mid-April. 'I remember it well. You don't forget special nights,' smiles Allan. 'We took a really good support as normal and even though it was more or less guaranteed that we were going up the boys were still desperate to do it in style and get a few goals and we managed to do that.' Superkev bagged four with Quinny inevitably getting in on the act as a 5-2 win saw promotion mathematically confirmed with four games to go. I was fortunate enough to be in the tunnel after the match and saw Niall taking ultimate delight in smashing up the boards that said Nationwide Division One. Sunderland were no longer members and those boards were a thing of the past, albeit ever the gentleman, Niall later paid for new ones at Bury.

Three nights later at Barnsley Superkev paraded a party-piece curler into the top corner for the TV cameras as another win was racked up. From the end of January, 14 of the final 17 games were won, with the other three drawn. The final day brought fourth-placed Birmingham City to Wearside. Skipper Ball had successfully appealed against a suspension that would have ruled him out of the game where he was to lift the trophy, and with Sunderland trailing at half-time the other Superkev let his team-mates know he didn't intend to lift the silverware after a defeat. Appropriately enough, it was the Batman and Robin duo of Quinn and Phillips who did the business in the second half to end the glorious campaign on a high note.

Sometimes after a promotion there is an element of apprehension about whether the team will be good enough for the higher level, but in 1999 supporters relished the 105-point team being let loose on the Premiership. Unfortunately, a couple of weeks later midfield dynamo Lee Clark was pictured at Wembley supporting his home-town team Newcastle wearing an anti-Sunderland T-shirt. It was a momentary and stupid blemish by Clark who was never less than fully committed in red and white, but it was inevitably the end for the Tynesider. Between Sunderland winning the league and Newcastle losing the cup final Sunderland had played two end-of-season games, a testimonial for 1964 promotion winner Jimmy McNab and a game against Liverpool to celebrate 100 years of the Football League. Current champions Sunderland had been asked to stage the game with Liverpool, who had won the most titles. The Anfielders had won that match 3-2 in a game where Johnston had scored one of his trademark curlers from the edge of the box into the top corner.

Surely 'Magic' would take the FA Carling Premiership by storm? Unfortunately not. Like Clark he had played his last game for the club. Disputes over new contracts led to manager Reid freezing him and Bridges out.

Now an experienced manager himself, Allan reflects on what happened after the promotion season and says, 'Sunderland was unbelievable. It was probably the best part of my career. I loved it and I loved the actual area as well. The north-east has great people and it is an unbelievable club. Everything was going brilliantly and I got picked for Scotland while I was there. When we got promoted I still had a year on my contract so there was a long way to go. It's not as if I was a player who was going to go through the motions. I was going to give everything because you know how much the fans had got behind you and I would always give 100 per cent. That's what I find a wee bit frustrating, that I wasn't involved even though I had a year left on my contract.

'It's some club, isn't it? It's amazing how big it is – it's massive. It's similar to Glasgow, where I'm from. The supporters are born and bred into the club. You know what it's like. If they can turn it round it will be brilliant.' Interviewing Allan at a busy time while he was manager of Queen of the South, he still had as many questions for me about the modern Sunderland, itself an illustration of his continued passion for his former club.

Allan Johnston deserved the nickname 'Magic'. His trickery wasn't just for show, however; the end product was devastating. The 1999 team won the old Football League championship trophy for the second time in four years but Peter Reid had created two totally different teams, albeit some players (Ball, Bridges, Gray, Melville, Martin Scott and Martin Smith) played a part in both campaigns. The 1996 team that won Roker Park's last trophy and the 1999 cohort who won the Stadium of Light's first league title were totally different in approach. The 1996 team eked out results, whereas the 1999 side blew the opposition away. The flair of the 105-point team and the goal fest it produced – while conceding even fewer goals than the defensively tight 1996 side – was a tribute to Peter Reid and chairman Bob Murray, who in producing the Stadium of Light had provided the stage for glory.

2004/05 CHAMPIONSHIP CHAMPIONS

Striker Stephen 'Sleeves' Elliott formed a dynamic partnership with the experienced Marcus Stewart and guides us through the first of his pair of promotion seasons with Sunderland, this one coming under the leadership of Mick McCarthy.

AS IN 1999 Sunderland stormed to the second-tier title in the season following play-off penalty shoot-out disappointment. Mick McCarthy's men didn't manage the phenomenal 105 points of Peter Reid's Quinn and Phillips-inspired record breakers, but in amassing 94 points they achieved the second-highest points tally in the club's history, a feat that shouldn't be overlooked.

It was certainly a stark contrast to the dismal relegation of two years earlier when just two measly points had been taken from the last 20 games. None at all had come from the final 15. When the first two games back in the second tier had also been lost to take the 17-match sequence of defeats to within one of the all-time record set in Victorian times by Darwen, media vultures circled McCarthy's side ready to pounce, the manager at this point having lost all 11 league games he had been in charge of.

Turning the tide with a live TV victory at Preston, Sunderland had roared back. Having finished third they lost on penalties in the play-offs to a Crystal Palace side whose equaliser really should have been disallowed for a foul.

Without much in the way of money to spend, 'Mic Mac' went bargain hunting in the summer. He brought in a mixture of players from the lower leagues and some who hadn't yet quite cut it at the top level. Stephen Elliott was one of the latter. 'Looking back, my memory is everyone was coming from different pathways,' says Elliott, who quickly became known to one and all as 'Sleeves' – a nickname gained due to his habit of constantly saying 'Sleeves up?'

'I'd come from Manchester City who were a big Premier League club, although obviously they weren't as big as what they are now. I'd done my apprenticeship there and come through the academy, so for me coming to Sunderland was about trying to make my mark at first-team level. For other lads such as Liam Lawrence, he had already had a few seasons at Mansfield and he was stepping up a couple of divisions. Then you had Deano [Whitehead] coming from Oxford, which also meant moving up a couple of levels. It was good having younger lads around and there were players such as Chris Brown and Grant Leadbitter – who came in a little bit later – who were making their way through the Sunderland youth system. All that does help when you are wanting to get on with people at a new club.'

The season kicked off with defeat at Peter Reid's Coventry, his first match in charge there. The following Tuesday night Sleeves came off the bench with 15 minutes to make an impression on his home debut against Crewe. Elliott got off to the perfect start in front of his new fans with a well-taken goal in the final minute. 'It was great to get a goal so early. I'd scored a lot of goals at youth team level, including for Ireland in internationals, but to get a goal in my first home game for Sunderland against Crewe, obviously I was delighted. My mam and dad had both come over for the game, so that made it even more extra special. It is one of the few goals that I remember quite clearly in my own mind without having to look at old videos. Some games you don't really remember but in that one I remember making a run because I'd seen they had quite a high line. Wrighty [Stephen Wright] threw a ball down the line and I just kept running and running. Before I knew it I found myself in the box. Their centre-half came across and I feinted to shoot as he dived in, after which I managed to just slot it in down by the keeper. I was buzzing to get my first goal. It wasn't so much relief – I was just delighted to be able to do it while my mam and dad were over.'

It was to be the only win in the first six league games, all of the rest of that run seeing Sleeves come on as a sub, getting the equaliser in a home draw with early leaders Wigan. In contrast, Sunderland were at the other end of the table. After losing to Reading three days later the Lads languished in 17th place, a point away from the bottom three.

Ignition for lift-off came at Gillingham, where Elliott was restored to the starting line-up and scored with a header in a resounding 4-0 victory which saw Marcus Stewart score a hat-trick. It sparked a run of four successive victories ending with a 1-0 win at Leeds which propelled Sunderland up to fourth, Sleeves having scored his first brace in a home win over Preston.

The win at Gillingham was the first of 13 in 18 league matches up to Christmas, by which time Sunderland sat third, level on points with second-placed Ipswich and a point behind Wigan, each of whom had a game in hand. Reading trailed the Wearsiders by two points but a seven-point gap had opened up between Sunderland and Sheffield United in fifth position.

Boxing Day brought the biggest gate of the season so far, over 43,000 against Leeds, who belied their 19th place by inflicting a 3-2 loss with one of the goals coming from Brian Deane, who by the end of the campaign would be helping Sunderland to get over the line.

Despite the disappointment, two days later Sunderland moved into the automatic promotion places for the first time, Wigan having lost both their Christmas games. A 2-1 win for McCarthy's men at Nottingham Forest saw both Sleeves and Stewart on the scoresheet. It was the start of a run of four goals in six league games for Elliott.

Stephen and Marcus would finish the season as the top two scorers, Elliott notching 15 in the league and another in the League Cup, while Stewart would edge him as top scorer with 16 in the league plus one more in the FA Cup, that cup goal being one of three Stewart scored from the penalty spot. Behind them no one else reached double figures, although cult hero Julio Arca managed nine.

The win at Forest was only the third – and surprisingly last – time both Elliott and Stewart scored in the same game during the promotion season. In 40 of the 46 games both featured, with at least one of them scoring in 23 of the fixtures. In the promotion seasons of 1987/88 and 1989/90, the G-force of Gabbiadini and Gates scored in 24 league games between them (with five fixtures where they both netted) in 1987/88 and in 20 league games in 1989/90, when both found the back of the net in the same game twice, in addition to the celebrated play-off game at Newcastle where the G-force blew away Newcastle.

Sleeves and Stewart were never known as the 'S-force' but perhaps they should have been. Like Gates and Gabbiadini they were a duo without a traditional target man in the style of Quinn and Phillips. Both former heroes at Ipswich, Gates and Stewart were wily, experienced goal poachers with the Teddy Sheringham-like ability to drop off and play their partner in. Sleeves was like Gabbiadini in that he had the pace to leave defenders in his slipstream (as with that home debut goal against Crewe) and the intelligence to know where and when Stewart was going to feed him. That is not to say that either partnership was about a maker and taker of goals because, other than in Gates's last two seasons when Marco far outscored the veteran Eric, they scored almost identical numbers with Gabbiadini and Elliott providing their fair share of assists for Gates and Stewart.

'I'd say it was pretty natural,' says Sleeves of his partnership with 'Stewy'. 'We weren't the biggest two forwards in the world so there was no point the lads lashing balls up around our neck. People might say we weren't the most exciting Sunderland team but we tried to play. If you analyse the games, in some of those we played some really good football.'

Indeed, another comparison between the teams of the G-force and S-force was in the managers. Both Denis Smith and Mick McCarthy were known as big, tough, kick-it-as-far-as-you-can centre-halves who took no prisoners, but both produced football teams at Sunderland who liked to get the ball down and play.

'We worked on interchanges and had midfield runners as well,' Elliott explains. 'Marcus Stewart was a very clever footballer. Playing alongside him, I learned quite a bit off him that year in terms of starting positions and getting your body across defenders, winning free kicks and so on. We linked up quite well and I was a little bit disappointed the following season when Marcus went. I thought he could have hung around for another year maybe. Not necessarily playing regularly but just having that level of experience in and around the dressing room. Everyone got on well with him as he mixed well with everyone.'

McCarthy did have a plan B in addition to Elliott and Stewart. The season started and ended with a target man being employed. Kevin Kyle played in the first half-dozen league games when Elliott was mainly coming off the bench, while Brian Deane made four substitute appearances in the last five games of the campaign, becoming the club's oldest debutant when 58 days beyond his 37th birthday. In addition, Chris Brown (son of Alan, who was third-top scorer in the 1979/80 promotion season) started 13 games and came off the bench 24 times, the most important of his five goals securing a 1-0 win over Coventry in mid-March as the season approached its business end.

That victory over the Sky Blues took Sunderland to the top of the table where they would stay until the end of the season. After that fleeting glimpse of being in the top two after the end of the calendar year win at Forest, the Black Cats had been third throughout January and most of February, before a narrow home win over Cardiff saw them leapfrog Ipswich on goal difference and be level on points with leaders Wigan. At this point the top three had pulled ten points clear of fourth-placed Derby but, of course, one of the clear best three sides in the division were going to be condemned to the play-offs, which Sunderland had suffered in the previous year.

There were seven games left and Sunderland still had to go to both Wigan and Ipswich. After a comfortable 3-1 win at QPR, Wearside descended on rugby town Wigan. Having had fewer than 13,000 for the previous weekend's home game with play-off contenders West Ham, Wigan had their biggest gate of the season for the midweek visit of Sunderland, a sell-out 7,400 away following seeing the gate top 20,000. 'I remember we had the whole stand opposite the dugouts packed out. The fact that they had travelled in such massive numbers, especially for a midweek game, made me think this is a really big club,' says Sleeves, who was on the bench, coming on for the last eight minutes in place of Stewart, who had scored the only goal of the game as early as the third minute. 'I remember the goal because they felt the ball had gone out of play before Lennie [Liam Lawrence] crossed it over to Stewy. That result gave us a really big chance of going up into the Premier League. We didn't play particularly well I don't think but it was a big game and it was all about getting the three points going into the last period of the season.'

Sunderland seemed to be motoring but hit a red light in the next game at home to Reading. Leading through a Julio Arca strike with quarter of an hour to go, they lost to two late Dave Kitson goals on a day when Norway international goalkeeper Thomas Myhre went off injured to be replaced by Michael Ingham.

Ingham dropped a corner for Richard Naylor to open the scoring midway through the next match, which was the crunch game at Ipswich. The Tractor Boys were five points behind Sunderland but victory over the Lads combined with winning their game in hand would take them above McCarthy's men, albeit there was also a five-point gap to Wigan with four games left. Nonetheless, back-to-back defeats at this stage of the season could have been calamitous. At 0-0 ex-Ipswich striker Stewart had missed with a penalty and it looked like it wasn't going to be Sunderland's day.

Three minutes after falling behind Sunderland made a double substitution, Elliott and Deane coming on. Within two minutes the pair combined for Sleeves to equalise. 'Big Brian Deane got me in. He headed the ball back across for me and I just managed to get ahead of Kevin Horlock and get my head on it at the back post.' With six minutes to go the turnaround seemed complete when Carl Robinson volleyed past Kelvin Davis, who would sign for Sunderland in the summer. However, it was another future Sunderland man who had the last word, Darren Bent levelling in the 89th minute.

The result left Sunderland on the cusp of promotion. Ipswich boss Joe Royle was magnanimous in his praise, saying afterwards, 'Their movement and running in midfield was excellent … We are fortunate to get a point. Sometimes you have to hand the opposition credit and Sunderland were excellent. They are a good unit.'

Good unit or not, there was still work to be done before promotion was assured. As Leicester came to the Stadium of Light McCarthy took the bold move of dropping Ingham and bringing in 17-year-old goalkeeper Ben Alnwick. As he picked the ball out of the net just five minutes into his debut fears of a second successive home defeat were palpable. Alnwick, however, rose to the occasion with two terrific saves, one from David Connolly, who two years later would be Sunderland's top scorer as promotion was won again. Promotion still had to be won here and was. Stewart equalised midway through the first half before centre-back Steve Caldwell majestically headed the winner after half-time. 'Other than Stevie's goal I don't remember too much about the game to be honest,' says Elliott, who came off the bench for the closing stages. 'I just remember the night out afterwards! It gets to a stage of the season where you think, "We're close now", but getting over the line is always the hardest part and it becomes more of a relief than anything. We were really confident at that stage that we were going to go up but when it's finally achieved it's a little bit of a relief when you can finally just enjoy it a little bit. There was a good few nights out after it when Stevie would tell us about his million-pound header. That's my most vivid memory of it – Stevie telling us he'd scored the most expensive header in Sunderland's history! At the time it would have been.'

Those celebrations couldn't start until a few minutes after referee Mike Jones's final whistle blew. The players gathered in the tunnel waiting for news of Ipswich's result at Elland Road. If the Tractor Boys could beat Leeds, Sunderland would not yet be mathematically sure of promotion. As it happened Darren Currie missed a last-minute open goal for Ipswich, who could only draw to give Wearside the best result involving Leeds since 1973.

Promotion was the priority but the next job was to secure the title. The following Friday night Sunderland took to the field at

Alan Pardew's West Ham, who were desperate for the points as they sought a play-off place. 'It was a great night,' remembers Sleeves. 'I didn't start. We went behind [to a Marlon Harewood goal just before half-time] and then Julio scored a second-half equaliser. When I came on I got what is one of my favourite goals for Sunderland. Our fans were packed in behind that goal at the Boleyn Ground, which was a ground I always liked playing at. There was always a good feeling around the place because it had that old school feeling about it. To score the winning goal there to win the championship in my first season made me think what a good season it had been for my first at the club. I felt I was really part of something special and to manage to score the goal that clinched the league was a great moment.'

Elliott's winner three minutes from time tied up the title with a game to spare and equalled the club record of 13 away wins for a season. Mick McCarthy doesn't always get the praise he deserves for the transformative job he did in some style at Sunderland. Anyone in football needs a thick skin and after his experiences as manager of the Republic of Ireland, McCarthy's was thicker than most. Known for his dry sense of humour, 'Mic Mac' informed the London press, 'I keep hearing we are not the best side in the Championship but I think that when people read the papers in the morning they will find that we are.'

A capacity crowd enjoyed a festival-like finale as Carl Robinson scored the only goal of the final game against Stoke, with the players subsequently enjoying an open-topped bus ride around the city, something Roy Keane would refrain from a couple of years later.

Stephen Elliott was named Young Player of the Year and the Republic of Ireland's Young Player of the Year in the 2004/05 promotion season, and would feature in a second promotion two seasons later when injury restricted him to 15 starts plus nine substitute appearances. 'In the second season I still felt like I'd played my part, although I'd picked up an injury and had an operation during that season. It was a bit of a disappointment personally but at the same time I played in over half the games. A lot of them were on the right wing and I didn't really play up front much but I felt I was developing as a footballer as I was learning about playing in a new position and we won most of the games I played, so I definitely didn't feel as if I wasn't part of it. When you are injured you want to play, but at the same time you have to look at the bigger picture. At that stage I'd become a Sunderland fan so you want the club to be back in the top division. Whenever the lads won a game I was as happy as anybody and would celebrate with the squad.

'I'd have only been 23 at that stage and for me personally it was two league winners' medals in three years. Obviously, we had come down in between but winning the league isn't an easy thing to do. To win the Championship twice in such a short space of time was a really great achievement by the club and a great way to bounce back. From a personal level I must have been thinking I'd win medals nearly every season, but when you stop playing you look back and think that some people never win anything after a long career in the game and I'd won two league medals by the time I was 23. I'm very proud of that as I am of the couple of medals I won at other clubs.'

Sleeves would go on to also win League One with Norwich and the Scottish Cup with Hearts, but having had such success and playing more games for Sunderland than any of his 11 clubs, does Sunderland mean more to him than simply being one of his former clubs? '100 per cent! You learn a lot about the area. I've got a lot of friends and people I'm fond of in the area and I know how much the football club means to them. My wife is from Sunderland and all my children were born in Sunderland, so now it's a lot more than just a former club. I was part of a successful period but even when I was playing elsewhere, if I had a weekend off I'd always come and watch Sunderland with my father-in-law. I was a Liverpool fan growing up but I would say that definitely Sunderland now is the team that I look out for even more than Liverpool. It's a fantastic football club and hopefully it can get back to playing at a level where the supporters deserve to be. The club will always be part of me.'

2006/07 CHAMPIONSHIP CHAMPIONS

*Defender Danny Collins describes a season that
began with the club being taken over, briefly saw
new chairman Niall Quinn double as manager and
then eventually led to promotion under Roy Keane.*

DANNY COLLINS played in the promotion seasons of 2004/05 and 2006/07. 'It was nice to be a part of them but if I'm asked which did I prefer, it would certainly be the second one because I felt more part of it in terms of the amount of games I played. In 2004/05 it was nice to come in and I played in 14 league games. I got my medal but you do feel like a bit-part player because the lads in the back four were doing well and you couldn't shift them out of the team.'

Collins had just 12 league appearances to his name when he signed for Sunderland from Chester, who had just re-entered the Football League after four years. 'I'd come up in the Carling Cup for Chester. Sunderland beat us quite comfortably that night two or three nil. Personally, I didn't have a bad game. I must have done something right because a few weeks later Mick [manager McCarthy] brought me up to the Stadium of Light. Obviously, with me signing from Chester the difference in terms of the size of the club – the stadium, the training ground, the fan base – everything about it was on a different scale. The club, I think, were about fifth in the league at the time, so I had to bide my time to get into the team. The settled back four were Gary Breen and Stevie Caldwell at centre-back and George McCartney and Stephen Wright at full-back. I was learning off Gary Breen and Stevie Caldwell. Stevie is the same age as me but he was ahead of me in terms of experience, so I was out on the training pitch learning from these guys which stood me in good stead for the years to come. For the likes of me and Neill Collins, who had come in from Dumbarton, we had to wait for the opportunities when they came around.'

Danny was called upon more the following season. He played in just over half the games as Sunderland were instantly relegated with a meagre 15 points. It was an incredibly tough year. The side he was part of lacked sufficient quality but were tremendous in terms of character. At any level, defeat after defeat knocks the stuffing out of teams and heavy defeats follow, yet the '15-point' side were never beaten by more than three and only twice conceded four. 'If you get relegated with 15 points it's with you for a long time,' admits Danny. 'When we got promoted Mick didn't get a lot of money to spend. It was a new chapter for a lot of us in terms of going into the Premier League, people like myself, Liam Lawrence and Deano [Dean Whitehead] had come up the season before from what is now League Two. There weren't too many hidings. We weren't going out and getting slapped 5-1. It was 1-0s and 2-1s a lot of the time. It was frustrating and disappointing but it was a learning curve for us in terms of us going forward from there.'

The summer of 2006 saw the Drumaville Consortium, led by Niall Quinn, take over from long-serving chairman Bob Murray. Hopes of a new dawn were high but, 'It didn't go well at the start. We lost the first four league games. It wasn't great but then Roy Keane took over. He brought lads in who he knew: Graham Kavanagh, Ross Wallace, Stan Varga, Liam Miller, David Connolly and Dwight Yorke, and then further down the line Jonny Evans and Danny Simpson. Sometimes you bring a lot of players in and it takes lads a long time to settle, but thankfully for us that year we sort of gelled and turned things round.

'Roy was unknown as a manager but everyone in the game knew his character as a player. Everyone knew the sort of standards he set and what he demanded from his team-mates. When he came in he brought that straight in. He wasn't particularly hands-on at the training ground. He left a lot of it to Tony [Loughlan, in 2021 still the long-term assistant to Sean Dyche at Burnley] to take care of the training but he was always out there watching. He would step in at times and say stuff if the training wasn't at it. He'd want the levels taken up a step and he'd join in now and then at the five-a-sides.

'Everyone had respect for him as a manager. He wanted things doing right on and off the pitch. Hotels and so on for away trips – everything was done right. He didn't like lads turning up late. That was his pet hate. If one or two boys were late he'd let them know about it.' That was never better seen than when he left Anthony Stokes, Márton Fülöp and Toby Hysén behind when they were late for the team bus for a late-season game at Barnsley. Asked the following week if the trio had subsequently been on time for training, Keane noted with his trademark glint of the eye, 'Of course – they brought the milk in.'

'It's a fine line as a manager – not that I've been one,' explains Danny. 'You have to have a good rapport with the players and be able to have a laugh and a joke. I think Mick was probably the best one in that respect. He'd like to have a laugh and a joke on the bus, but when it was time to work on the training pitch he would switch into that manager mode and it would be serious for that hour and a half or two hours or whatever, so that things were done right.

'On away trips Deano, myself, Dwight Yorke and the gaffer [Roy Keane] would have a game of cards and he'd have a laugh and a joke, but as soon as we got to the hotel or the ground for a game he goes into that Roy Keane mode, the sort of thing you see on *Super Sunday* where he takes that back step. At times he likes to keep himself to himself but I got on great with him.

'When he came in I came out of the team. We'd had that bad spell at the start of the season and he changed one or two things. I had a bit of a chat with him in his office where he said, "Where are you at?" and I told him I knew we hadn't had a good start but I was happy to stay and fight for my place, to which he said, "That's fine by me." I got back in the team a couple of weeks later and stayed in for the majority of the season. Players like myself and Deano were the type of players that I think you would associate with Roy because we were hard-working lads who would go out week in, week out and try and give our all, and I think that's what Roy's character as a player was about as well.'

Niall Quinn had signed off as a manager with a win over West Brom as Keane sat in the stands. An international break saw Keane installed. He began with a bang with terrific wins at Derby and Leeds, but just one point was taken from the next two games before Danny got his first chance under the new boss, helping to keep a clean sheet in a narrow win over Sheffield Wednesday. It was the first of 15 consecutive starts Danny made up to Christmas. During this period the team blew so hot and cold that as Santa arrived they were only 11th, ten points adrift of the automatic promotion spots.

Five January signings provided a telling injection of new blood. In particular, the arrival of Jonny Evans (on loan from Manchester United) and Carlos Edwards helped to get the promotion show on the road. 2007 started with a New Year's Day victory at Leicester. It was the first in a sequence of 14 wins and three draws in 17 league games. After a brief spell out of the side, Danny came back into the team as a sub in the second game of this run. He then was brought back into the starting line-up at Sheffield Wednesday where endless chants of 'Keano' to the tune of 'Hey Jude' failed to soften the manager's fury at two late goals being conceded after his team led 4-0. The team could start to make it better by not conceding a goal for the next four fixtures following Keane's rant about late defensive sloppiness.

A large part of this improvement in the defence was down to the blossoming partnership between new boy Evans and erstwhile right-back Nyron 'Nugsy' Nosworthy as a central defensive partnership – a combination that meant Danny Collins settled into the left-back berth, having previously switched between centre-back and left-back. 'Prior to Roy coming in I'd done a bit of both under Mick. In my Chester days I'd played as the left-sided defender in a back three, so at times I did get that licence to go forward, so it wasn't strange for me to go out and play left-back. To be fair I would probably say centre-half if asked which position I preferred to play but you want to be out on the pitch, so if asked to play left-back then, of course, I was happy to do so.

'With regard to "Nugsy" going to centre-back, Roy had assessed his game on the training ground and wanted him to keep things simple. He was a strong, quick lad and his job was to win the ball, not let anyone go past him and then give the ball to the lads who could play in front of him. With Jonny coming in during January alongside him, Jonny was more your ball-playing centre-half, so it was a case of letting Jonny do the ball-playing side of it.'

So often the partnerships that are remembered are attacking ones, such as the G-force of Gates and Gabbiadini, or Superkev and Quinny from the 1987/88, 1989/90 and 1998/99 promotions, but defensive partnerships can be just as important. Nosworthy and Evans became reminiscent of the great Jeff Clarke–Shaun Elliott duo from the 1979/80 promotion side, with Nosworthy the Clarke-like stopper while Evans was as good as Elliott on the ball, if not quite as quick.

With Danny at left-back and new recruit Danny Simpson – like Evans a January loan acquisition from Keane's old club Manchester United – the defence became a solid and dependable unit. Simpson was never on the losing side in the 14 appearances of his loan. Behind them the underrated but consistent goalkeeper Darren Ward, or sometimes Márton Fülöp, would add to the solid base the team had established.

With David Connolly scoring regularly in a team that largely shared the goals around, winning became a habit. 'When you are losing you go into the training ground on a Monday morning and it's quiet and there's a few mopey faces around the place. You've got to try and lift it, whereas on the flipside when you're on an unbeaten run, you go in and everyone can't wait to get out on the training pitch. You're looking forward to the next game coming around because you're going out there thinking you're going to win, rather like Liverpool no doubt were in 2019/20. It's just the flipside of football when you have that sort of consistency and the starting XI more or less picks itself unless you've got injuries or suspensions. It makes a manager's job easier. The confidence we had after Christmas was tremendous. We could see we were gaining on the teams above us and we timed it well to nick the lead off Birmingham.'

Managed by future Sunderland supremo Steve Bruce, Birmingham had emerged as Sunderland's major promotion rivals, along with Derby County. Only a controversial last-minute equaliser had denied Sunderland victory at St Andrew's. It was the middle game of a run of seven where the other six were all won. This was part of the 17-game unbeaten run that included a win at Cardiff, after which chairman Quinn ended up organising and funding taxis home for a plane-load of supporters after an airline mistook happiness for hooliganism and ejected a couple of fans from a plane in Bristol. Niall was on the plane with myself and other members of the club's media department. When he got off in solidarity with the supporters the rest of the red and white army followed, leading to the night of Niall's taxis. As I was being handed wads of cash at £500 a time, my job was to shepherd groups of four fans into taxis and send the drivers north. Many of the taxi drivers were from overseas and had no idea how far north they were headed. Niall himself didn't want to make anything of the incident but, of course, it became legendary.

After the unbeaten run unceremoniously ended at Colchester in the third from last game there were worries that Sunderland might blow their promotion chances. These fears were deepened in the following match as Burnley led in Sunderland's last home game.

The Clarets were managed by Steve Cotterill, who had been Howard Wilkinson's assistant in their ill-fated time at Sunderland. One of their goalscorers was Andy Gray, who had endured a terrible time in the 15-point team of the previous term. The visitors also included Steve Caldwell, who had scored the winner the last time Sunderland had won promotion but had been quickly discarded by Keane after starting the season with Sunderland. Burnley were a team with a point to prove.

At kick-off against the men from Turf Moor, Sunderland, Birmingham and Derby were in a three-horse race for two automatic promotion places. The Lads had one point more than Derby but one fewer than Birmingham. Fail to beat Burnley and control of the

Black Cats' own destiny was lost. With 11 minutes to go and the score tied at two all there came a goal in keeping with the magnitude of the occasion. 'I remember the build-up to Carlos's goal that won it,' says Danny. 'It was played out from the back until Daryl Murphy slotted it across to Carlos, who ran on to it and cracked it into the top far corner from about 25 yards. It was a great night. We had that character about us. There were games where towards the end of the match we kept on driving and kept on digging in when we had to and we would nick a goal here and there late on. It was good. We had a lot of momentum and took it to the end of the season.'

Two days later goals from Clinton Morrison and Mark Kennedy sealed Sunderland's promotion. Their strikes for Crystal Palace defeated Derby and mathematically secured Sunderland's elevation. Derby's defeat also secured Birmingham City's place back in the Premier League. Steve Bruce's Blues were favourites for the title but fluffed it with defeat at Preston, who were hoping for a place in the play-offs. Sunderland, meanwhile, made mincemeat of already-relegated Luton on their own patch. Watched by 'King' Charlie Hurley, the captain of Sunderland's first promotion team, Sunderland looked every inch the Championship champions. 'We went to Luton knowing we had to win and knowing that Birmingham had to win to deny us. We were 2-0 up in six minutes and went on to win 5-0 while Birmingham lost. It was nice to finish it but what I do remember is it was disappointing that they didn't have the trophy there.'

Believing that promotion was not something a club of Sunderland's stature should be marking with an open-topped bus ride, Roy Keane eschewed the celebration. Instead, the trophy was presented at a private function at Seaham Hall. 'We'd done it with Mick a couple of years before. I was only 24 and it was a good experience to drive through the middle of Sunderland with thousands of fans in the streets. We then had the disappointment of coming down again the year after and then we won the league again. I could see exactly where Roy was coming from. We didn't want to be seen as a yo-yo club like West Brom were at the time, bouncing between the Premier League and the Championship. Had we failed again the year after, we didn't want to have been celebrating by driving through the streets as it would have looked a bit silly in a way – so I have no qualms with that. At Seaham Hall we had our wives or girlfriends with us. There was a nice meal, there was a comedian on and a disco and stuff after, so it was great. We also had a video on a big screen showing the highlights of the season. It was a good experience.'

Danny went on to be both Sunderland and north-east Player of the Year in 2009. Like Len Ashurst, Dick Malone, Gary Bennett and Stephen Elliott, for example, Danny is not a native of Wearside but lives in the area after ending his playing days. 'Most ex-pros probably associate themselves or their career with one club and for me it is obviously Sunderland,' he says. 'I had more time than I had at any other club and my wife is from up in the north-east. I met her early on after I'd come to Sunderland and we've got two kids. The longer you are at the club the more you see what it means to the fans. They've all got their shirts on whatever day of the week it is. Once I moved back up to the area I'd go and watch games and I've got involved with a bit of media at the club, which I enjoy. Hopefully it'll be good to see Sunderland get back up into the Championship and ultimately into the Premier League.'

THE PLAYERS

In the player statistics the first figure relates to the number of league matches they started, the figure in brackets relates to substitute appearances and the third column relates to goals scored. There were no substitutes in Sunderland's first promotion season of 1963/64. Substitutes for league games were introduced in 1965/66. For example, in 1987/88 Reuben Agboola started 37 league games, came on as a substitute once and didn't score.

AGBOOLA, Reuben
Date of birth: 30 May 1962
Place of birth: Camden, London
Position: Defender

Promotion campaigns:
1987/88 league statistics: 37(1)-
1989/90 league statistics: 30(6)- Play-offs 3(-)-

Mobile, tough and ever popular, Reuben remains the first in the list of all Sunderland players alphabetically and was also the club's first player to be capped by an African country. Londoner Reuben won caps for Nigeria, the country of his father, debuting in April 1991 against Benin.

Agboola had come to Sunderland from Southampton where he had a strained relationship with Lawrie McMenemy. To his dismay McMenemy took over at Sunderland after Agboola arrived. Although he rarely played under his old Saints boss he became a regular player during his promotion seasons under Denis Smith.

———

AGNEW, Steve

Date of birth: 9 November 1965
Place of birth: Shipley, Yorkshire
Position: Midfielder/winger

Promotion campaign:
1995/96 league statistics: 26(3)5

A good-quality footballer who played 70 times in total for Sunderland, the prematurely balding Agnew was an important figure as Endsleigh Division One was won in 1995/96. A creative and industrious midfielder, he chipped in with a handful of goals, including the first of the season and one in an important win over Derby.

Starting with over 200 games for Barnsley, Agnew went on to play over 50 for Leicester and York as well as Sunderland, in addition to a handful of games for Blackburn and Portsmouth. Finishing his playing career with Gateshead, he had spells as caretaker manager at Middlesbrough and Sheffield Wednesday, before becoming part of Steve Bruce's coaching staff at Newcastle United.

———

AISTON, Sam

Date of birth: 21 November 1976
Place of birth: Newcastle
Position: Winger

Promotion campaigns:
1995/96 league statistics: 4(10)-
1998/99 league statistics: (1)-

Long-striding teenage winger Aiston was a useful impact sub in the 1995/96 promotion campaign but was only called upon once in the record-breaking 1998/99 season, coming off the bench in a 3-1 win at Grimsby. In between his contributions to the pair of promotions Sam suffered a serious injury to his knee ligaments. Nonetheless, he went on to have a long career, having his lengthiest spell at Shrewsbury.

ALNWICK, Ben

Date of birth: 1 January 1987
Place of birth: Prudhoe
Position: Goalkeeper

Promotion campaigns:
2004/05 league statistics: 3(-)-
2006/07 league statistics: 11(-)-

Debuting on the day promotion was won in 2005, teenager Alnwick showed great character to excel after being beaten in the opening minutes. Previously on the bench 27 times in the league that season, Alnwick went on to impress in the win at West Ham that wrapped up the title and kept his first clean sheet before over 47,000 on the day the trophy was presented after Stoke were beaten.

After getting five games in the Barclays Premiership, Ben made 11 early-season appearances as the second tier was won for the second time in three seasons in 2006/07. He was then transferred to Spurs in a deal that saw Márton Fülöp move in the opposite direction. Alnwick went on to make ten or fewer league appearances for ten clubs, mainly on loan, before topping 80 games with both Peterborough and Bolton.

ANDERSON, Stan

Date of birth: 27 February 1934
Place of birth: Horden
Position: Midfielder

Promotion campaign:
1963/64 league statistics: 10-

One of the most popular players of the era, local lad Stan had more than held his own in the 'Bank of England' team of the 50s, when Sunderland signed many of the country's top stars. During the 60s Stan became the only player from the club to be capped by England with whom he was also part of the 1962 World Cup squad.

Anderson donned his regular number 4 shirt for the opening ten games of the 1963/64 promotion season, before a sensational and controversial transfer to local rivals Newcastle United who he captained to promotion the following season. As he made clear on numerous occasions Stan did not want to move from Wearside to Tyneside, but his stature and popularity was such that he was still given a hero's welcome when he returned to Roker Park at the end of the promotion season for his testimonial match, as a Newcastle player.

Rejected by Middlesbrough as a youngster, Anderson later joined Boro from Newcastle, becoming the first player to captain all of the north-east's big three clubs. It was at Middlesbrough where Stan moved into management. Subsequently, he also managed AEK Athens, Doncaster Rovers and Bolton Wanderers, as well as holding numerous assistant manager and coaching positions. Stan's biography was published in 2010.

———

ANGELL, Brett

Date of birth: 20 August 1968
Place of birth: Marlborough

Position: Centre-forward
Promotion campaign:
1995/96 league statistics: 2(-)-

Brett Angell played the first two games of his promotion season but was quickly discarded by Peter Reid, regardless of scoring in a League Cup tie in between those two league appearances. Angell was one of those forwards who often did well against Sunderland but had a tough time on Wearside. A promotion winner with Southend United, Stockport County, Preston North End and Walsall, he won a Player of the Year award with the Shrimpers and was inducted into the Hatters (Stockport not Luton) Hall of Fame.

———

ARCA, Julio
Date of birth: 31 January 1981
Place of birth: Buenos Aires
Position: Midfield/left-back

Promotion campaign:
2004/05 league statistics: 39(1)9

Few players of the Stadium of Light era can rival 'Julioooo' for popularity. Cult hero status was achieved on the back of an awesome amalgamation of ability and attitude. A FIFA Under-20 World Cup winner with Argentina in 2000/01 at the end of a season when he had been Sunderland's Young Player of the Year, in the 2004/05 campaign he was third-top scorer behind the front two of Marcus Stewart and Stephen Elliott.

Arca went on to become equally popular at Middlesbrough where he became Player of the Year and later, after injury saw him drop into non-league, he won the FA Vase at Wembley with South Shields in 2017. All in all, the boy from Argentina became a hero at three north-east clubs.

———

ARMSTRONG, Gordon
Date of birth: 15 July 1967
Place of birth: Newcastle
Position: Midfielder

Promotion campaigns:
1987/88 league statistics: 36(1)5
1989/90 league statistics: 46(-)8 Play-offs 3(-)-
1995/96 league statistics: -(1)-

Only six players have ever exceeded Gordon Armstrong's total of 416 appearances for Sunderland. Vastly underrated, Gordon became the first midfielder since 1973 cup-winning skipper Bobby Kerr to register a half-century of league goals for Sunderland, Armstrong's tally totalling 61. One of those came on the night Sunderland sealed the third division championship against Northampton. More famously, four years later his last-minute winner in an FA Cup quarter-final replay with Chelsea was one of the greatest headers in the club's history.

Heading is not usually an attribute prominent in midfielders but it was one of Gordon's strengths, along with the wholehearted commitment of a passionate lifelong Sunderland supporter and a passing range considerably better than most people gave him credit for. As promotion was won in 1990 Armstrong was not only ever present but started 58 of the 59 games in all competitions, missing only the solitary game in the Zenith Data Systems Cup. In contrast, in 1995/96 his only league appearance came as a sub on the opening day, and after three more occasions when he was an unused sub he finally moved on.

———

ARNOTT, Kevin

Date of birth: 28 September 1958
Place of birth: Gateshead
Position: Midfield

Promotion campaign:
1979/80 league statistics: 37(-)8

The maestro of the 1980 promotion winners, 'Ossie' Arnott oozed class. So often, Sunderland supporters bemoan the lack of a midfield creator but this was never the case when Arnott was in the side. Usually operating in or around the centre circle, 'Ossie' dictated play and sparked danger whenever he approached the penalty area.

Possessing brilliant ball control and able to effortlessly deliver perfectly weighted passes, Arnott was Sunderland's answer to Glenn Hoddle. During the season, as Sunderland won the prestigious

Daily Express five-a-side championship at Wembley Arena, Arnott ran the show and finished as top scorer. Seven of his eight league goals in the promotion season came at home, crucially one of these opening the scoring in the match that sealed the return to the top flight.

After leaving Sunderland he should have continued to have a career with stellar clubs but with all respect to those Kevin later played for, he did not do himself justice. He did, however, do well for Sheffield United where he signed for Ian Porterfield.

——

ASHURST, Jackie

Date of birth: 12 October 1954
Place of birth: Coatbridge
Position: Defender

Promotion campaigns:
1975/76 league statistics: 20(1)-
1979/80 league statistics: 2(1)-

No relation to Len Ashurst of the 1964 side, Jackie hailed from Coatbridge, as did his 1975/76 promotion-winning team-mate Billy Hughes. Jackie was one of five players to play in the promotion campaigns of 1975/76 and 1979/80, albeit his appearances in the latter of those two triumphs were rare. At his best in central defence, he was versatile enough to operate in either full-back position or as a defensive midfielder but came to the fore alongside Bobby Moncur for the final 11 games of 1975/76 following injury to Jeff Clarke. The final three of his 166 appearances for the club came in the early part of the 1979/80 campaign before he signed for his former coach Stan Ternent at Blackpool.

——

ASHURST, Len

Date of birth: 10 March 1939
Place of birth: Liverpool
Position: Defender

Promotion campaign:
1963/64 league statistics: 42 1

'Lennie the Lion' was a tough-tackling left-back who went on to become the club's outfield-appearance record holder, and later returned to manage the club. Ever present in the promotion season, Len scored one of his rare goals with a thunderbolt of a shot in the derby with Newcastle in a 2-1 home win.

An England youth international, he debuted in September 1958 in the same game as his 1964 promotion-winning team-mates Cec Irwin and Jim McNab. Len remained an important part of the first-team scene until 1970.

Moving down the A19, Ashurst bridged the move into management as player-manager of Hartlepool United. Later, he managed Gillingham, Sheffield Wednesday, Newport County and Cardiff City, before taking over at Sunderland in 1984. In Len's season at Sunderland he took them to the League Cup Final for the first time but was unable to stop the team being relegated, along with Norwich, who defeated his side at Wembley.

Ashurst went on to manage in the Middle East, as well as having a second stint at Cardiff and managing in non-league. In total he had over half a century in the game, spending many years as a match delegate, assessing refereeing in the Premier League. In the week of his 70th birthday, Len released his self-penned autobiography, *Left Back in Time*. He was inducted into the Sunderland Hall of Fame at its inaugural dinner in 2019.

———

ATKINSON, Brian

Date of birth: 19 January 1971
Place of birth: Darlington
Position: Midfield

Promotion campaigns:
1989/90 league statistics: 11(2)- Play-offs -(1)-
1995/96 league statistics: 5(2)-

A teenager in the 1989/90 campaign, in some respects Brian was a 'mini-me' of Paul Bracewell. Like his mentor, Atkinson was an accomplished midfielder who was good at always being available for a pass and equally adept at delivering a simple but effective ball. He went on to play for England at Under-21 level and in the 1992 FA Cup Final, as well as coming off the bench in the 1990 play-off final.

The 1995/96 promotion season was Brian's final one at the club. After making the last of his club total of 169 appearances in December, he went on loan to Carlisle in the January of that season and moved to Darlington in the summer.

ATKINSON, Paul
Date of birth: 19 January 1966
Place of birth: Chester-le-Street
Position: Winger

Promotion campaign:
1987/88 league statistics: 21(1)3

'Atky' was a speed-merchant winger who won 18 England Youth caps and scored in the top flight as a 17-year-old. The promotion campaign was Paul's most productive in terms of appearances but it was also his last as he moved on to Port Vale, where unfortunately injury brought his career to an end when he was only 25. A talented player, but for injury Paul would most likely have risen back up the leagues.

BALL, Kevin
Date of birth: 12 November 1964
Place of birth: Hastings
Position: Centre-back/midfield

Promotion campaigns:
1995/96 league statistics: 35(1)4
1998/99 league statistics: 42(-)2

Captain of two title-winning promotion teams, 'Bally' was a superb skipper. A leader who had the ability to ensure he got the maximum out of his team-mates, Kevin ruled with a rod of iron on and off the pitch. The ultimate professional, he accepted nothing less than the best of attitudes from everyone. A central defender in his early years, after playing in the 1992 FA Cup Final, Ball moved into the centre of the park where his drive and determination proved invaluable. Underrated as a player as people focussed on his often crunching tackling, Kevin's passing could be telling while he would also chip in with an occasional goal. Player of the Year in 1990/91, Bally also took the Supporters' Association award on four occasions.

————

BENNETT, Gary

Date of birth: 4 December 1961
Place of birth: Manchester
Position: Defender

Promotion campaigns:
1987/88 league statistics: 38(-)2
1989/90 league statistics: 38(-)3 Play-offs 3(-)-

A legendary figure at Sunderland, 'Benno' is fifth on the all-time club appearances list – two of the four men above him being goalkeepers. Player of the Year in 1986/87 and 1993/94, Gary was always a player who gave his all. Moreover, while he was not Sunderland's first black footballer, he was the first to command a regular place across a season. Undoubtedly, he did more than anyone to combat racism in football on Wearside. This is something he has continued to do into the 2020s through his work with Show Racism the Red Card, while for many years he has summarised Sunderland games for local BBC radio.

Twice a promotion winner on Wearside, Gary was a regular in the side who won two promotions in three years. Usually utilised at centre-back, Gary also played at right-back or in midfield, but wherever he was playing the sight of Benno bombing forward was always a sight to behold.

BERTSCHIN, Keith
Date of birth: 25 August 1956
Place of birth: Enfield
Position: Forward

Promotion campaign:
1987/88 league statistics: 14(11)5

The one person who the G-force partnership of Eric Gates and Marco Gabbiadini didn't work for. Gabbiadini had been signed to dovetail with Bertschin but Keith broke his jaw in their second game together, and by the time he was fit again the chemistry between Gates and Gabbiadini had become apparent. The consequence was Bertschin became the stand-in striker rather than the main man.

Notably Keith contributed the first and final goals of his promotion campaign. The first was more important than the last. By the time he wrapped up a 4-1 victory at Rotherham promotion was long since secured. On the other hand, his opening-day goal at Brentford was the club's first third-tier goal and the winner as he got the season off to a positive start. Over two decades later Keith returned to the club as reserve team manager during the reign of Steve Bruce.

___

BOLTON, Joe
Date of birth: 2 February 1955
Place of birth: Birtley
Position: Defender

Promotion campaigns:
1975/76 league statistics: 34(-)1
1979/80 league statistics: 22(-)-

As a teenager Joe Bolton played in the first two games of the 1973 FA Cup run having debuted late the previous season. By 1975/76 he had established himself as the first-choice left-back and would go on to play over 300 games for the club. In an era when tackles could be tackles, Joe was amongst the hardest of hard men and unsurprisingly took on cult hero status at Roker Park. Although Joe scored a dozen goals in total for the club, the only one in either of his successful promotion campaigns came on the final day of the 1975/76 season when he opened the scoring against Portsmouth on the day the title was secured. The following season Joe won the club's first official Player of the Year award.

——

BRACEWELL, Paul

Date of birth: 19 July 1962
Place of birth: Heswall
Position: Midfielder

Promotion campaigns:
1989/90 league statistics: 36(1)2 Play-offs 3(-)-
1995/96 league statistics: 38(-)-

England international Bracewell was in his second and third spells with the club when he won his two promotions. A player of exceptionally high calibre, 'Brace' had partnered 1996 (and 1999) promotion-winning manager Peter Reid in the Everton midfield as they won the top flight and European Cup Winners' Cup in 1984/85. That season Paul also played in the FA Cup Final, one of four he lost in his career, including 1992 when he skippered Sunderland. Injuries hampered his playing days but he was still good enough to be a major figure in two red and white promotions, as well as one in black and white when he joined Newcastle in 1992.

——

BRADY, Kieron

Date of birth: 17 September 1971
Place of birth: Glasgow
Position: Midfielder/winger

Promotion campaign:
1989/90 league statistics: 9(2)2 Play-offs -(-)-

Kieron Brady made his debut during his promotion season with all but two of his appearances in that campaign coming in the final couple of months. Possessing outrageous natural talent and the flamboyance to enjoy using it, Brady was a player who could attract people to the game and was robbed of what could have been an outstanding career due to popliteal artery syndrome that seriously curtailed what he had to offer. He played his part in promotion with a winner at Bradford a week after his standout performance against West Ham, when in a sensational display he won a penalty after a Billy Hughes-like slaloming run into the box, and also scored a bicycle kick in a thrilling 4-3 victory.

___

BREEN, Gary
Date of birth: 12 December 1973
Place of birth: Hendon, London
Position: Centre-back

Promotion campaign:
2004/05 league statistics: 40(-)2

Captain of the 2005 Coca-Cola champions, Republic of Ireland international Breen was a commanding presence on the pitch and at the training ground. A good communicator, Gary was brought to the club by his former international manager Mick McCarthy and delivered, as he helped to instil a winning mentality as the club was turned around after a dismal relegation in 2003 and play-off penalty defeat in 2004.

___

BRIDGES, Michael
Date of birth: 5 August 1978
Place of birth: North Shields
Position: Forward

Promotion campaigns:
1995/96 league statistics: 2(13)4
1998/99 league statistics: 13(17)8
2004/05 league statistics: 5(14)2

Michael Bridges played in three Sunderland teams that won promotion by winning the league. The trio of titles came at different stages of Mickey's career, with him coming off the bench more often than he started on each occasion. Breaking into the team as a 17-year-old in 1995/96, his sublime first touch illustrated he was a class act, while his two-goal burst as a late sub to turn potential defeat into victory against Huddersfield showed his finishing ability.

Three seasons later Mickey was still a youngster but by then capable of being a regular starter. He stood in successfully for Kevin Phillips when Superkev was injured, but a fit Phillips meant 'Stickman' Bridges's path to the first team was blocked. By the time of the 2004/05 campaign Michael was trying to rebuild a career that had been badly affected by injury, following a big-money move to Leeds.

_____

BROWN, Alan

Date of birth: 22 May 1959
Place of birth: Easington
Position: Forward

Promotion campaign:
1979/80 league statistics: 29(4)9

The 'Easington Express' was a speed merchant. Later a loan player with Newcastle United, Brown scored both goals at St James' Park in a drawn League Cup second leg and completed a hat-trick of sorts by scoring in the successful shoot-out. That derby victory boosted belief in a promotion season in which Alan contributed a real hat-trick in a home win over Oldham.

1979/80 was Brown's best season at Sunderland. Twenty-five years to the month after Alan's heroics at St James', his son Chris made his debut for Sunderland. He went on to add 69 appearances to the family tally in addition to his dad's 127.

_____

BROWN, Chris

Date of birth: 11 December 1984

Place of birth: Doncaster
Position: Forward

Promotion campaigns:
2004/05 league statistics: 13(24)5
2006/07 league statistics: 10(6)3

The son of 1980 promotion winner Alan Brown, Chris featured in both promotions in the middle of the first decade of the century. In 2004/05 he featured in the last 37 games of the season, his most important goal being a winner against Coventry. Two seasons later he scored Sunderland's first goal under the management of Roy Keane, but soon found himself moved on.

———

BUCHANAN, Dave

Date of birth: 23 June 1962
Place of birth: Newcastle
Position: Forward

Promotion campaign:
1987/88 league statistics: 1(-)-

Dave Buchanan was subbed in an early-season home draw with Bury during the promotion season. It was to be his last appearance for Sunderland and his solitary outing of the promotion campaign. While Buchanan joined Sunderland from Blyth Spartans, he had begun with Leicester City, becoming the Foxes' youngest-ever league player at the age of 16 years and 192 days when he made his first appearance on the same day as Gary Lineker.

———

BUCKLEY, Mick

Date of birth: 4 November 1953
Place of birth: Manchester
Position: Midfielder

Promotion campaign:
1979/80 league statistics: 17(2)2

Mick Buckley was a busy central midfield player. A crisp passer of the ball, Mick was always on the move and a master at making interceptions. A former England Under-23 international, his face stared down from the cover of his first club Everton's programme on the night Sunderland were relegated in 1977, but he played his part in taking the Lads back up.

Although he didn't play as much as he had in the previous season, which had been his first at the club, Buckley never weakened the team by being included and indeed started the last four games when his contribution was invaluable. He weighed in with a couple of goals, one in an early-season home win over Cambridge, with the other in a late-season 5-0 thrashing of Watford. More importantly, his winner on the final day of the season against Manchester City two seasons later was the goal that secured Sunderland's safety.

Sadly, Mick passed away in 2013, a month before what would have been his 60th birthday.

―――

BUTLER, Paul

Date of birth: 2 November 1972
Place of birth: Manchester
Position: Centre-half

Promotion campaign:
1998/99 league statistics: 44(-)2

Along with the arrival of goalkeeper Thomas Sørensen, centre-half Paul Butler was largely responsible for a tremendous reduction in the number of goals scored from the season before his arrival when Sunderland lost in the play-offs to his promotion season when only 28 goals were conceded in 46 games, compared with 50 the season before.

A physically imposing defender, Butler was a commanding focal point of the defence, providing the platform for what was an exceptionally exciting side. He earned his first international recognition with a Republic of Ireland B cap in the promotion season and went on to win his solitary full cap the following year. Having sold him to Wolves for £100,000 more than the £900,000 it had cost to buy him from Bury, Paul's 2003 promotion with Wolves netted Sunderland an additional £100,000. He had also been a promotion winner with the Shakers. Elsewhere in his career Paul played over 100 games for both Leeds and Rochdale.

――――

CALDWELL, Steve
Date of birth: 12 September 1980
Place of birth: Stirling
Position: Centre-back

Promotion campaigns:
2004/05 league statistics: 41(-)4
2006/07 league statistics: 11(-)-

Steve Caldwell headed the goal that sealed promotion in 2005 when he had been a regular member of the side in his first season at Sunderland after his move from Newcastle. Two seasons later he featured in another promotion season, but this time as a peripheral member of the team. The final game of his Sunderland career came at the end of December after which he was transferred to Burnley, where he signed for former Sunderland assistant manager Steve Cotterill and went on to win promotion as play-off winners in 2008/09.

A Scotland international, he went on to become assistant manager of Canada, having finished his playing days with Toronto.

――――

CARTER, Darren
Date of birth: 18 December 1983
Place of birth: Solihull
Position: Midfield
Promotion campaign:
2004/05 league statistics: 8(2)1

On loan from Birmingham City between 18 September and 6 December in his promotion season, during that spell he was an unused sub four times as well as appearing in ten league games during a run of 14 consecutive fixtures. A goal on his debut in a home win against Preston got Carter off to a great start, but it wasn't the first time he had netted for the home side at the Stadium of Light. He had scored for England Under-20s against Italy in 2002. It was one of 11 caps he won at that level, three of which came at the 2003 FIFA World Youth Championships in the UAE.

As a team-mate of Stern John, he scored the decisive penalty to take Birmingham into the Premier League in 2002 with victory over Norwich City at the Millennium Stadium. Having made 85 Premier League appearances early in his career for Birmingham and West Brom, Darren subsequently played extensively in the Championship. His final six seasons saw him operate in the National League with his last two clubs, firstly Forest Green Rovers before being named in the National League Team of the Season with his home-town Solihull Moors in 2018/19.

CARTER, Tim

Date of birth: 5 October 1967
Place of birth: Bristol
Position: Goalkeeper

Promotion campaigns:
1987/88 league statistics: 1(-)-
1989/90 league statistics: 18(-)- Play-offs -(-)-

Tim Carter debuted at Wembley in the Mercantile Credit League Centenary tournament against Wigan during the 1987/88 promotion season, before the former Bristol Rovers man made his league bow against Bristol City in the penultimate home game, a 0-1 defeat that was the only one of the final eight games that wasn't won.

Two years later a broken arm suffered by number one Tony Norman enabled Tim to have an extensive run in the team, during which he kept four clean sheets. Tragically, Tim apparently took his own life in 2008.

CHAMBERLAIN, Alec
Date of birth: 20 June 1964
Place of birth: March, Cambridgeshire
Position: Goalkeeper

Promotion campaign:
1995/96 league statistics: 29(-)-

Alec Chamberlain was a reliably consistent goalkeeper whose positional sense meant that spectacular saves were the exception rather than the rule. As Craig Russell explains in his chapter on 1995/96, Chamberlain lost his place to the outstanding on-loan Shay Given after manager Peter Reid felt his keeper should have done better for a cup goal at Manchester United. Nonetheless, when Given was injured at the business end of the season Chamberlain slotted back in seamlessly and kept five successive clean sheets, by which time promotion was secured. He went on to be twice Watford Player of the Year, winning back-to-back promotions with the Hornets with whom he played over 250 times after leaving Sunderland. He also became the first player to win the League Cup while with Sunderland – something he did while on loan from SAFC to Liverpool in 1995 as an unused sub. Earlier in his career he played over 100 times for each of Colchester (where he was Player of the Year) and Luton.

———

CHISHOLM, Gordon
Date of birth: 8 April 1960
Place of birth: Glasgow
Position: Defender

Promotion campaign:
1979/80 league statistics: 12(1)-

Like Shaun Elliott, 'Chis' could operate in midfield as well as in his best position of central defence. He went on to play over 200 games for the club and later returned in the Stadium of Light era to head up the scouting system, but in the promotion campaign he was on the fringe of the side.

All but four of his league appearances in 1979/80 came in the opening two months of the season but he did return for three late fixtures. One of these came in the final match where promotion was clinched against West Ham United. Only on the losing side three times in his dozen league starts, Gordon later was unfortunate to deflect home an own goal in the 1985 Milk (League) Cup Final as Sunderland lost 1-0 to Norwich.

——

CLARK, Ben

Date of birth: 24 January 1983
Place of birth: Shotley Bridge, Co. Durham
Position: Defender/midfield

Promotion campaign:
2004/05 league statistics: 1(1)-

Capped 38 times at various youth levels with England, local lad Clark came to Sunderland having started with Manchester United. Extremely highly rated as a young player, Ben only ever started three league games for Sunderland. He was in the side on the opening day of the promotion season but was subbed at Coventry before coming off the bench in the next match. They would be his last league games for the club, his final appearance coming in the League Cup at Crewe the following month.

He went on to play 162 league games for Hartlepool and another 280 in total for non-league Gateshead, who he also managed.

——

CLARK, Lee

Date of birth: 27 October 1972
Place of birth: Wallsend
Position: Midfield

Promotion campaign:
1998/99 league statistics: 26(1)3

Forever tainted by his unsavoury departure from Sunderland after being photographed wearing a T-shirt bearing a derogatory statement about Sunderland while supporting his home-town team Newcastle at the FA Cup Final, Lee Clark was actually an excellent player in red and white.

Despite breaking his leg on the opening day of his Wearside promotion season, 'Clarkie' still managed to play in over half the games. In his one previous campaign at the Stadium of Light he had been ever present. Despite his lack of dress sense, Clark had a superb football brain on the pitch, his creativity and vision in the centre of the park being a vital cog in the machine that saw the team produce a record 105 points.

An England Under-21 cap, he made over 200 league appearances in two spells at his beloved Newcastle and 149 for Fulham, also winning promotion to the top flight with both of his other clubs. He went on to manage Huddersfield, Birmingham, Blackpool, Kilmarnock, Bury, Blyth and, from March 2021, Sudanese club Al-Merrikh SC.

————

CLARKE, Clive
Date of birth: 14 January 1980
Place of birth: Dublin
Position: Left-back

Promotion campaign:
2006/07 league statistics: 2(2)-

Republic of Ireland international Clarke was recruited by Niall Quinn as the Drumaville Consortium took control of the club, a reported fee of £400,000 bringing him from West Ham. Clive came on as a sub in the second game of the season and started the third, only to be substituted. Following the international break, new manager Roy Keane gave him the full game in what proved to be the heaviest defeat of the season at Preston. In the next match he was used as a sub in a defeat at Stoke, after which he would twice more be named on the bench without being called upon.

In August 2008 Clarke suffered a cardiac arrest at half-time in a game at Nottingham Forest while on loan from Sunderland to Leicester City. He then retired on medical grounds.

____

CLARKE, Jeff

Date of birth: 18 January 1954
Place of birth: Hemsworth
Position: Defender

Promotion campaigns:
1975/76 league statistics: 31(-)-
1979/80 league statistics: 39(-)1

Jeff Clarke was a major part of two promotions but missed the run-in on both occasions through injury. In 1975/76 he was a mainstay of the side for the first 31 games before missing the final 11. Four seasons later he was stretchered off in the penultimate game at Cardiff and missed the final match where promotion was clinched against West Ham. He had played every game until mid-April when he missed a couple of matches before coming back into the side.

A commanding centre-half, Clarke had come to Sunderland in the summer of 1975 from Manchester City as a makeweight in the deal that took England centre-half Dave Watson to City. The ultimate compliment that can be paid to Jeff is that Watson wasn't missed! In his first promotion season Clarke partnered the veteran Bob Moncur, while in 1979/80 he often played alongside Rob Hindmarch but was at his best when partnered with Shaun Elliott.

____

COADY, Mike

Date of birth: 1 October 1958
Place of birth: Dipton
Position: Defender

Promotion campaign:
1979/80 league statistics: -(1)-

Mike Coady was a really promising player when he debuted as a teenager at Leeds in 1977, but his only appearance of his promotion year was his sixth and final game for Sunderland.

Coady's contribution lasted just 21 minutes as he came off the bench for goalscorer Alan Brown as Sunderland forlornly tried to come from behind at Preston North End in mid-February. It was to be the last loss of the campaign. Coady left at the end of the season to sign for Carlisle manager Bob Stokoe, who knew him from his time at Roker Park.

———

COLLINS, Danny

Date of birth: 6 August 1980
Place of birth: Chester
Position: Centre-back/left-back

Promotion campaigns:
2004/05 league statistics: 6(8)-
2006/07 league statistics: 36(2)-

Chester City had only just been promoted back into the Football League when Danny Collins played at the Stadium of Light for them in a League Cup tie early in the first of his two Sunderland promotion-winning seasons. Commanding and assured, Collins caught Mick McCarthy's eye and shortly afterwards was added to the Black Cats squad.

In a defensively sound side, he made the team sheet in half of the games of the season, including nine times as an unused sub. Personal progress meant that he started over half the games the following season in the Premier League and as promotion was won again in his third campaign, Danny was a key player and regular starter. He went on to be the club's Player of the Year in 2008/09 and became immensely popular, as players do if like him they combine commitment with quality. In 2020/21 he began summarising games on SAFSEE, offering excellent insight along with evident passion for the club where he played his best football.

COLLINS, Neill

Date of birth: 2 September 1983
Place of birth: Irvine
Position: Centre-back

Promotion campaigns:
2004/05 league statistics: 8(3)-
2006/07 league statistics: 6(1)1

No relation to Danny, like his namesake, Neill played in both promotions during the opening decade of the century. Although both centre-backs, they were very different in style. Neill wanted to bring the ball out of defence more than Danny, but would also take more chances and be in danger of being caught in possession.

In 2004/05 at one point Neill got three successive league outings during which only one goal was conceded. On the only other occasion he got back-to-back games no goals were leaked. In 2006/07 Neill got a run of five starts in the space of six games as Roy Keane took over from Niall Quinn (Neill scoring the last goal of Quinn's brief reign as manager), but the first and last of that little run brought 3-1 losses at Southend and Ipswich. His final appearance came in a home defeat to Cardiff when future Sunderland striker Michael Chopra scored twice.

Collins went on to win promotion with Wolves under Mick McCarthy and at Leeds under Simon Grayson. Neill himself went on to become head coach of Tampa Bay Rowdies.

———

CONNOLLY, David

Date of birth: 6 June 1977
Place of birth: Willesden, London
Position: Striker

Promotion campaign:
2006/07 league statistics: 30(6)13

Top scorer as promotion was won under Roy Keane, David Connolly had first attracted Sunderland's attention many years before he came to the Stadium of Light. An experienced player who had appeared against Sunderland for Leicester on the day the previous promotion was sealed, Connolly played a big part in the club's ninth promotion.

One of a host of transfer-deadline incomings, David didn't get off the mark until his tenth appearance but then started to find the net regularly, one of his best goals helping to rescue a point at Burnley. That was the only one of the 13 games in which Connolly scored that wasn't won.

The return game with the Clarets was one of two games where Connolly scored with a penalty. In what was the last home game of the season he had already had a spot kick saved when he showed the character to take and convert another penalty at a crucial stage of the game. In a long career where he played for 13 clubs, including two in the Netherlands, promotion at Sunderland was one of his two successes. He also won the Football League Trophy with Southampton, although he only played the last five minutes against Carlisle at Wembley.

———

COOKE, John
Date of birth: 25 April 1962
Place of birth: Manchester
Position: Forward

Promotion campaign:
1979/80 league statistics: 4(-)1

Seventeen-year-old striker John Cooke played an important part in the promotion season, although he only played four times. His winner on his second appearance – three months after his debut – was crucial. Cooke's winner came on a foggy day against Luton at Roker Park.

During the promotion season he was also part of the six-man squad who won the Daily Express five-a-side championships at Wembley Arena. Capped by England at youth level, 'Cookie' remained at Sunderland until 1985 and then returned in 1993 as kit manager, a role he carried out until 2020. His son Jay Turner-Cooke played for Sunderland at Under-18 level.

COOKE, Terry

Date of birth: 5 August 1976
Place of birth: Marston Green
Position: Winger

Promotion campaign:
1995/96 league statistics: 6(-)-

Only on loan at Sunderland for a month from Manchester United, shortly after his loan Terry returned to Roker to play for England Under-21s against Croatia in April 1996, one of four caps he won at that level. Earlier in the season he had made his Premiership debut for his parent club who he had also played for in the UEFA Cup before coming to Sunderland. He went on to cross Manchester in a £1m move to City and later played in America, Australia and Azerbaijan as he sought his 'A' game.

CORNER, David

Date of birth: 15 May 1966
Place of birth: Sunderland

Position: Defender
Promotion campaign:
1987/88 league statistics: 4(0)0

Sunderland won the FA Cup ten days before David's seventh birthday. He may have dreamed of playing in a cup final for his home-town team but when he did as a teenager it became a nightmare. 'Cornered' was the name of Jeff Brown's stage play written about David, who was forever linked with an error that led to the only goal of the 1985 Milk (League) Cup Final loss to Norwich. During the promotion season of 1987/88 he featured in a four-game run in the autumn, the first three being won. He also played in a 7-1 Sherpa Van Trophy win over Rotherham in which he scored. Capped by England at Under-20 level, Corner went on to gain winners' medals in the Vauxhall Conference and Division Four with Darlington.

CORNFORTH, John

Date of birth: 7 October 1967
Place of birth: Whitley Bay
Position: Midfielder

Promotion campaigns:
1987/88 league statistics: 8(4)2
1989/90 league statistics: 1(1)- Play-offs -(-)-

John Cornforth made a total of 38 appearances for Sunderland, 14 of them coming in two promotion seasons. A debutant on the day Sunderland bowed out of the top flight in 1985, a sequence of six successive starts in the autumn of the 1987/88 campaign included a brace of goals in a home win over York. The second half of the season often saw him on the bench. Cornforth was an unused sub seven times in addition to the times he actually played. In 1989/90 he came off the bench on the opening day of the season, but appeared in only one other league game, a Boxing Day start in a narrow home win over Oxford. He went on to have a successful career elsewhere, being capped for Wales and managing Exeter City, Newport County and Torquay United between 2001 and 2006.

————

CRADDOCK, Jody

Date of birth: 25 July 1975
Place of birth: Redditch
Position: Centre-back

Promotion campaign:
1998/99 league statistics: 3(3)-

Jody Craddock was on the team sheet for half the games in the 105-point promotion season. Unfortunately, 20 of these 23 occasions saw him named as sub, with him being called into action just three times. He also made five League Cup appearances in the same season but in his other five campaigns at the club he always played between 20 and 40 times. He went on to win promotion again with Wolves under his old Sunderland manager Mick McCarthy and staged a testimonial match against Sunderland at Molineux. During his career he became a noted artist and made that into a successful post-playing career.

___

CROSSAN, Johnny

Date of birth: 29 November 1938
Place of birth: Londonderry

Position: Forward
Promotion campaign:
1963/64 league statistics: 42 22

Top scorer in the club's first-ever promotion team, Sunderland benefited when a controversial life ban in British football was lifted and the Wearsiders were able to bring him back from playing in Belgium with Standard Liège, for whom he had played in the 1962 European Cup semi-final against Real Madrid. One of four ever-presents in the promotion season, he also played all six FA Cup games, scoring five times, including twice in the quarter-final away to Manchester United. A sharp and incisive finisher, Crossan got more than one goal in a game on eight occasions in league and cup during the promotion season, including doing so in four successive games early in the new year. A biography, *The Man They Couldn't Ban*, was published in 2020.

___

CULLEN, Tony

Date of birth: 30 September 1969
Place of birth: Gateshead
Position: Winger

Promotion campaign:
1989/90 league statistics: 5(11)- Play-offs -(-)-

A teenager at the start of his promotion season, local winger Cullen struggled to impress the crowd but always gave his best. As well as appearing 16 times in the league during 1989/90 he was also an unused sub ten times. He was at least named on the bench in every game up to mid-November but thereafter became an increasingly peripheral figure.

——

CUMMINS, Stan
Date of birth: 6 December 1958
Place of birth: Sedgefield
Position: Forward

Promotion campaign:
1979/80 league statistics: 26(-)12

Little Stan Cummins – he was 5ft 6in – was a big player in the promotion team. Once tipped to be English football's first £1m player by his Middlesbrough manager Jack Charlton, Cummins cost Sunderland a club record £300,000 in November of his promotion season. Stan supplied an instant return on the investment with goals in his first two games and just kept scoring. A four-goal haul against Burnley and strikes both home and away to Newcastle were amongst Stan's special contributions, but he saved his best moment of the season for the cracking individual goal to make it 2-0 in the crunch final game with West Ham.

A year later Cummins again came up trumps on the final day of the season, scoring the winner at Liverpool as Sunderland stayed up on the final day. Things soured when he chose to leave for Crystal Palace on a free transfer after a contractual problem, but he returned to Roker for a second spell before finishing his career in America, where he continued to live after his playing days.

——

CUNNINGHAM, Kenny
Date of birth: 28 June 1971
Place of birth: Dublin
Position: Centre-back
Promotion campaign:
2006/07 league statistics: 11(-)-

A veteran Republic of Ireland international who had played at the 2002 FIFA World Cup, Cunningham was signed by Niall Quinn, a team-mate from that tournament. The last of Kenny's appearances in his only season at Sunderland came before the turn of the year with the team in the bottom half of the table.

Retiring after his time on Wearside, Cunningham had previously played 250 league games for Wimbledon and over 130 for each of Millwall and Birmingham City. His promotion season at Sunderland was his only honour.

DEANE, Brian

Date of birth: 7 February 1968
Place of birth: Leeds
Position: Centre-forward

Promotion campaign:
2004/05 league statistics: -(4)-

Brought in to help get Sunderland over the line, two of Brian's late-season appearances came in the games promotion and the title were secured, on both occasions against former clubs of his in Leicester and West Ham. Best known for his time with Sheffield United with whom he scored the Premier League's first-ever goal against Manchester United in 1992, Deane also scored the first competitive goals at Leicester's new stadium in 2002 and won three England caps.

DELAP, Rory

Date of birth: 6 July 1976
Place of birth: Sutton Coldfield
Position: Midfielder

Promotion campaign:
2006/07 league statistics: 6(-)-

Rory Delap became famous as the man with the enormously long throw, although this weapon in the armoury of a schoolboy javelin champion was never seen at Sunderland – although he only played 13 games in total for the club. Rory played the opening six games of the season under Niall Quinn (including a cup tie) but was discarded by Roy Keane after playing in Keane's first match.

By the following month he was shipped out on loan to Stoke. Allowed to play against Sunderland, he broke his leg on his home debut for Stoke against his parent club but stayed in the Potteries to not only recuperate but go on to be a key factor in their effective era under Tony Pulis. He went on to win promotion and play in an FA Cup final for Stoke, having also been a promotion winner with Carlisle earlier in his career.

———

DICHIO, Danny
Date of birth: 19 October 1974
Place of birth: Hammersmith, London
Position: Centre-forward

Promotion campaign:
1998/99 league statistics: 16(20)10

Being the back-up to Niall Quinn was an enormously tough task for anyone at Sunderland, where a host of forwards were signed to replace Quinn only to be big disappointments. 'Mellow-D', however, did as well as anyone could have expected when injury to the talismanic Niall gave Danny plenty of opportunities to play his part in promotion. Indeed, he was in the team or on the bench in all but four of the 46 league games and was third-top scorer behind Quinn and Superkev in the league. Later a promotion winner with West Brom in 2002, his success with the Baggies brought an extra £100,000 into the SoL coffers as part of his transfer deal. He went on to play against Sunderland for Millwall in the 2004 FA Cup semi-final.

———

DOYLE, Steve
Date of birth: 2 June 1958
Place of birth: Port Talbot

Position: Midfielder

Promotion campaign:
1987/88 league statistics: 31(1)1

An industrious but never popular player, Doyle had been signed by Lawrie McMenemy having impressed against Sunderland on the opening day of the previous season for Huddersfield. Doyle was the kind of player who did a lot of the unsung 'donkey work' tirelessly working for the team, but was rarely elegant in possession.

DUNN, Barry
Date of birth: 5 February 1952
Place of birth: Sunderland
Position: Winger

Promotion campaign:
1979/80 league statistics: 15(5)2

Plucked from non-league football with Wearside League Blue Star, willowy winger Barry Dunn made his debut during the promotion campaign. Always looking to take his man on, get to the line and whip a cross in, Barry contributed a couple of goals which helped earn points in draws at Watford and Bristol Rovers.

A former gas board employee, Barry had allegedly supposedly been accused of stealing pipes from the gas board. Consequently, he was forever plagued by the joke, 'When are Sunderland getting under-soil heating?' to which the answer was, 'When Barry Dunn gets the pipes.' He took the jibes with a smile and remained a popular figure in the press area in the Stadium of Light era.

EDWARDS, Carlos
Date of birth: 24 October 1978
Place of birth: Patna, Trinidad
Position: Winger

Promotion campaign:
2006/07 league statistics: 15(-)5

Carlos Edwards scored a goal to rival any other in a promotion season. Picture the scene: the last home game of the season, live on TV on a Friday night at the end of the first season under the Drumaville Consortium, just a year after Sunderland had been relegated with a record low 15 points. In a dramatic game v Burnley with the score standing at 2-2 with ten minutes left, the ball was played out from almost on Sunderland's own goal line. Spotting Carlos steaming up the right flank, Daryl Murphy played a ball into Edwards's path. Carlos took a touch before hitting a shot of such precision, power and importance it must be amongst the favourite goals of any Sunderland supporter.

Edwards had been signed in the January transfer window and had been a key figure in transforming the season with a fabulous second half of the season run. He appeared intent on creating his own goal of the season competition as he lashed in a succession of screamers. A cracking lad as well as a tremendous winger, if Edwards never did anything else but score that goal against Burnley his place in red and white folklore would still be assured.

Part of the PFA Team of the Year in the Championship that season, he had twice previously been in PFA Teams of the Year and had been a promotion winner with Wrexham in 2003.

———

ELLIOTT, Dave
Date of birth: 10 February 1945
Place of birth: Tantobie, Co. Durham
Position: Midfield
Promotion campaign: 1963/64
1963/64 league statistics: 5 0

Half-back Dave Elliott stood in for Jim McNab for five consecutive matches in the spring of 1964. McNab's injury meant that Elliott also got to play in all three games of the epic FA Cup quarter-final with holders Manchester United. Just a teenager at the time, this was his first season in senior football. Dave's third league appearance came in a derby at Newcastle, who he subsequently joined in 1966.

———

ELLIOTT, Robbie

Date of birth: 25 December 1973
Place of birth: Gosforth
Position: Defender

Promotion campaign:
2006/07 league statistics: 7(-)-

Signed on an initial one-month contract after being released by Newcastle United, Elliott's deal was then extended until January, after which he moved on to Leeds United. A six-game run bridged the changeover from Niall Quinn to Roy Keane as manager, after which he got another game at Stoke in mid-October only for him to be involved in the accidental collision that caused the leg break to Rory Delap, who was playing for Stoke on loan from Sunderland.

Following his short spell at Sunderland Elliott had similarly brief stints with Leeds and Hartlepool, having previously had two extensive spells with Newcastle either side of a four-year period at Bolton.

———

ELLIOTT, Shaun

Date of birth: 26 January 1957
Place of birth: Haltwhistle
Position: Defender

Promotion campaign:
1979/80 league statistics: 41(-)4

An outstanding player. When used in midfield Elliott was always a more than useful footballer, but he was always at his best in central defence, especially when partnered with Jeff Clarke. The pair had a terrific understanding, Clarke usually attacking the ball with Elliott covering. Pace and composure were Shaun's most obvious assets but there was also a steely determination that made it difficult for forwards to get the better of him.

Elliott missed just one late-season fixture during the promotion season, making 51 appearances in total. He chipped in with four goals including a brace in the penultimate home game as Watford were beaten 5-0. Unlucky not to win a full England cap, one of his three England B caps came at Roker Park in a match against Spain in the March of the promotion push.

ELLIOTT, Stephen

Date of birth: 6 January 1984
Place of birth: Dublin
Position: Forward

Promotion campaigns:
2004/05 league statistics: 29(13)15
2006/07 league statistics: 15(9)5

Stephen Elliott won two promotions in his first three seasons at Sunderland and went on to win another promotion with Norwich in 2010, lift the Scottish Cup with Hearts in 2012 and become a full international.

Known to all as 'Sleeves', he was a live-wire forward full of pace and with an ability to maximise that. In 2004/05 his partnership with Marcus Stewart saw the duo score 31 league goals between them, with Sleeves's high points including scoring the winner at West Ham that sealed the Coca-Cola Championship title.

Two years later Sleeves was used mainly in a wider position but still chipped in with some telling goals, not least one at Wolves that kept honours even in the first managerial meeting of Roy Keane and Mick McCarthy in the wake of their 2002 FIFA World Cup furore.

ENTWISTLE, Wayne

Date of birth: 6 August 1958
Place of birth: Bury

Position: Forward

Promotion campaign:
1979/80 league statistics: 2(-)-

By his own admission Wayne Entwistle was something of a rough and ready centre-forward rather than a cultured player, although he won England caps at youth level. Having started the season by scoring away to his home-town club Bury in the Anglo-Scottish Cup, he played in the third and fourth league games and the first leg of the League Cup meeting with Newcastle, before leaving to follow his old Roker boss Jimmy Adamson to Leeds.

During the previous season Entwistle had been second-top scorer with 14 goals in all competitions, a figure that included a hat-trick against Bristol Rovers and most famously the 'other' goal on the day Gary Rowell scored a hat-trick in a 4-1 win at Newcastle.

――――

EVANS, Jonny
Date of birth: 3 January 1988
Place of birth: Belfast
Position: Centre-back

Promotion campaign:
2006/07 league statistics: 18(-)1

One of the advantages of having Roy Keane as manager was his ability to procure loanees from Manchester United. Jonny Evans came from Old Trafford in the January transfer window and was partnered in central defence with erstwhile full-back Nyron Nosworthy. The result was that the pair dovetailed beautifully as the campaign was transformed with their axis providing the basis for a second half of the season push to promotion. While Nosworthy was the stopper, Evans was the ball player. Still a teenager at the time, he played with the composure expected of an experienced pro, so much so that it came as no surprise he went on to enjoy a career as a Premier League thoroughbred, not least in a second loan at Sunderland following promotion.

FINNEY, Tom

Date of birth: 6 November 1952
Place of birth: Belfast
Position: Winger

Promotion campaign:
1975/76 league statistics: 7(1)1

The namesake of one of England's greatest ever players, Sunderland's Tom Finney became a Northern Ireland international while at the club. His promotion season was his second campaign at Roker.

Having been very much on the fringe in his first season, he was called upon in December, getting a goal against Hull on Boxing Day in his first home league appearance in 11 months. From there he featured strongly until early March, scoring against Hull again in the FA Cup before dropping out of the team after the FA Cup quarter-final defeat to Crystal Palace. He left Sunderland for Cambridge during the summer after elevation to the top flight.

———

FOGARTY, Amby

Date of birth: 11 September 1933
Place of birth: Dublin
Position: Forward

Promotion campaign:
1963/64 league statistics: 3 1

Having been at the club since 1957, the Republic of Ireland international made the final three of his 174 Sunderland appearances in September 1963, notching his 44th and final goal in a home win over Manchester City. Sold to Hartlepool United in November of the promotion campaign for their record fee of £10,000, he became the first player to win an international cap while with the Teesside outfit.

FÜLÖP, Márton

Date of birth: 3 May 1983
Place of birth: Budapest
Position: Goalkeeper

Promotion campaign:
2006/07 league statistics: 5(-)-

Brought in from Spurs – initially on loan – during the promotion season, the 6ft 5in keeper conceded just twice in his five appearances, one of those outings coming on the final day of the season as the title was confirmed with a 5-0 win at Luton. From his arrival until the end of the season, he spent every other game bar one as an unused sub. The exception was at Barnsley when he was one of three players left behind by Roy Keane when he was late for the team bus. The son of a Hungarian international who played at the 1978 FIFA World Cup and appeared in the film *Escape to Victory* with Pele and Bobby Moore, very sadly the immensely likeable Márton passed away in 2015 at the age of just 32.

_____

GABBIADINI, Marco

Date of birth: 20 January 1968
Place of birth: Nottingham
Position: Forward

Promotion campaigns:
1987/88 league statistics: 35(-)21
1989/90 league statistics: 46(-)21 Play-offs 3(-)1

Marco Goalo was the main man of Sunderland's two promotions in three years. Plucked as a raw youngster from manager Denis Smith's old club York, Gabbiadini hit the post on his debut before proceeding to score twice in each of his next three games. Establishing a seemingly near telepathic understanding with ex-England veteran Eric Gates, the pair became renowned as the 'G-force' – Gates typically providing the service for the pace of Gabbiadini to power through opposition defences. As Sunderland strode to the third division title in 1988, Gates almost matched Gabbiadini on the goals trail – Marco providing many of the assists – while en route to promotion to the top flight in 1990 the pair's partnership was never better seen than when they combined for 'Gabbers' to wrap up victory in the play-off semi-final at Newcastle.

____

GABBIADINI, Ricardo

Date of birth: 11 March 1970
Place of birth: Newport
Position: Forward

Promotion campaign:
1989/90 league statistics: -(1)- Play-offs -(-)-

Marco's younger brother's only first-team appearance for the club came at Leeds in October 1989. Coming on for Marco, the pair came close to being the first brothers to play alongside each other for the club since Billy and John Hughes did on John's solitary Sunderland appearance in 1973.

____

GATES, Eric

Date of birth: 28 June 1955
Place of birth: Ferryhill
Position: Forward

Promotion campaigns:
1987/88 league statistics: 42(-)19
1989/90 league statistics: 34(2)6 Play-offs 3(-)1

Former England international Eric Gates was one of the big names brought in by Lawrie McMenemy, only to have an initially unsuccessful time in his native north-east. Gates had scored twice in the relegation play-off second leg with Gillingham, but it was after the arrival of Marco Gabbiadini that Eric showed the Wearside public the quality that had made him such a dynamic part of Bobby Robson's successful Ipswich side from earlier in the decade.

The pair hit it off with a natural understanding. Gates supplied the panache and Gabbiadini brought the pace. It is easy to think that Eric was the maker with Marco the taker of goals. That was largely true in the 1989/90 promotion campaign but as Division Three was won two years earlier, Gates scored just one goal fewer than Gabbiadini in league and cup. Nonetheless, the latter campaign saw both of the G-force score as they blew away Newcastle in the famous play-off victory at St James'.

———

GIBB, Tommy
Date of birth: 13 December 1944
Place of birth: Bathgate, Lothian
Position: Midfield

Promotion campaign:
1975/76 league statistics: 5(1)1

Gibb was a long-serving player with Newcastle who came to Sunderland at the start of the club's second promotion season but never established himself. In total he appeared in 13 games over two seasons before moving on to Hartlepool. During his promotion season at Roker Park Tommy appeared in the opening six league games, scoring in a 2-0 win over Fulham. He had also scored in the early-season Texaco Cup, but after dropping out of the team at the start of September managed only a couple of other occasions where he was named on the bench without being utilised.

———

GILBERT, Tim
Date of birth: 28 August 1958
Place of birth: South Shields
Position: Defender

Promotion campaign:
1979/80 league statistics: 8(-)1

Tim Gilbert stood in for Joe Bolton at left-back during the autumn. He did so well that when first-choice Bolton returned to the team, manager Ken Knighton found a place for Gilbert in midfield. Never out of his depth in the middle of the park, Gilbert rewarded the faith of his boss with the winner at home to Chelsea in his first game of the term in that role.

Industrious, determined and a good user of the ball, Tim was predominantly on the fringe of the first team during his time at Roker Park but never let anyone down when selected. Although he appeared in 13 games in all competitions during the promotion season, his final outing of the campaign came in early November.

At the tender age of just 36, Tim passed away suddenly. His son Peter went on to have a long league career and gain caps at Under-21 level for Wales.

———

GIVEN, Shay
Date of birth: 20 April 1976
Place of birth: Lifford, County Donegal
Position: Goalkeeper

Promotion campaign:
1995/96 league statistics: 17(-)-

Although he became a legend at Newcastle United, Given won a trophy in his brief loan on Wearside. He was outstanding at Sunderland. Plucked from Blackburn reserves by Peter Reid, teenager Shay was thrust into a debut at Leicester two days after being introduced to his new team-mates. He proceeded to keep the first of 12 clean sheets in his 17 games. His agility and sure-handedness made him an instant favourite that not even over a decade on Tyneside could totally diminish.

———

GRAY, Frank
Date of birth: 27 October 1954
Place of birth: Castlemilk, Glasgow

Position: Defender
Promotion campaign:
1987/88 league statistics: 12(22)-

One of McMenemy's big-name veterans, Scottish international Frank Gray had won the European Cup with Nottingham Forest and played in the final of the same competition for Leeds United. Frank's brother Eddie had played against Sunderland in the 1973 FA Cup Final, while his son Andy made a scoring debut for Sunderland in 2005, albeit that was Gray junior's only goal for the club.

Father Frank was named in the matchday squad of 13 in 45 of the 46 league games and featured in a total of 34 games despite starting only a dozen times. Often utilised as a sweeper, as befitting the high standards he had operated at earlier in his career, Gray brought a level of composure and class when he played and started regularly at the higher level the following season.

———

GRAY, Martin
Date of birth: 17 August 1971
Place of birth: Sedgefield
Position: Midfielder

Promotion campaign:
1995/96 league statistics: 4(3)-

A handful of appearances during the 1995/96 promotion season brought Martin Gray's five seasons as a first-teamer to a close. A hard-working player who was versatile enough to play at full-back as well as across the midfield, Martin was best as a destroyer. Later finishing his playing career with Darlington, Martin gave the Quakers great service, managing them from 2012 to 2017 as they worked their way back up the pyramid following their demise as a league club.

GRAY, Michael

Date of birth: 3 August 1974
Place of birth: Sunderland
Position: Midfielder/left-back

Promotion campaigns:
1995/96 league statistics: 10(6)-
1998/99 league statistics: 36(1)2

Promotion probably meant as much to Michael Gray as any player ever. A Castletown lad who is in the top ten of all-time appearance makers, Mickey infamously saw his decisive penalty saved in the 1998 play-off final with Charlton. A year later, after he had been an outstanding figure in the record-breaking 105-point season, as Gray approached the towering West Stand on the lap of honour, the Chumbawumba hit 'I get knocked down, but I get up again' blared from the PA. It was poignancy personified; Mickey had responded to despair with determination and shown the quality that had seen him break into the full England side.

His left-flank partnership with Allan 'Magic' Johnston was one of several fabulous combinations in a promotion side that is the only one to rival the first-ever promotion team of 1964 in the popularity stakes. Michael had already featured as an ever-present in the 1995/96 promotion but in 1998/99 he had that double reason for unbridled joy.

———

GRAY, Phil

Date of birth: 2 October 1968
Place of birth: Belfast
Position: Striker

Promotion campaign:
1995/96 league statistics: 28(4)8

Nicknamed 'Tippy' (because of his initials), Phil was one of three Grays who played in the 1995/96 Endsleigh Division One title-winning team. The Northern Ireland international won the last three of the 13 caps he won with Sunderland during the promotion season, scoring in the last two of them. A clever forward with good touch and movement, he scored in an FA Cup replay against Manchester United in addition to his eight league goals in what was the last and least productive – in a personal sense – season at Sunderland.

———

GREENWOOD, Roy

Date of birth: 26 September 1952
Place of birth: Leeds
Position: Winger

Promotion campaign:
1975/76 league statistics: 13(3)2

Bought for just £5,000 less than the club's record signing of the time (Pop Robson), Roy Greenwood arrived from Hull City for £140,000 just over two weeks after playing against Sunderland on Boxing Day. Already cup-tied having played for the Tigers against Plymouth a week before signing for Sunderland, Greenwood had to sit out the run to the FA Cup quarter-final and so couldn't play against his former club in the fourth round.

However, he was able to play a part in the promotion run-in, appearing in all but two league games from his transfer to the end of the campaign, on those occasions being an unused substitute. He got a couple of goals in a home win over Southampton and remained Hull's top scorer at the end of the season, having scored nine times in league and cup before Christmas.

———

HALL, Gareth

Date of birth: 20 March 1969
Place of birth: Croydon
Position: Defender

Promotion campaign:
1995/96 league statistics 8(6)-

Wales international Hall arrived from Chelsea where he had played 194 times in all competitions, but he was never convincing at Sunderland. He did, however, feature in most games in the second half of the season after debuting as a sub at Derby just before Christmas. He went on to top 50 appearances in Sunderland colours, often featuring as a defensive midfielder as well as in his primary back-four position.

———

HALOM, Vic

Date of birth: 3 October 1948
Place of birth: Burton upon Trent
Position: Forward

Promotion campaign:
1975/76 league statistics: 21(3)4

A cult hero at Sunderland, centre-forward Halom was a real handful for any defender and a character supporters simply loved. Vic played to the crowd with a smile and a glint in his eye, but this would have counted for nothing if he hadn't been able to do the business on the pitch. He had been signed during the cup-winning campaign of 1972/73 by Bob Stokoe, who he had earlier played for at Charlton. During the 1975/76 season Halom's Sunderland career came to an end. His four goals all came in home wins, the last two in a November visit of Nottingham Forest. Almost all of his appearances in the promotion season came before Christmas. In 1992 Halom stood as a candidate in the General Election for the Liberal Democrats in Sunderland North, finishing third.

———

HARDWICK, Steve

Date of birth: 6 September 1956
Place of birth: Mansfield
Position: Goalkeeper

Promotion campaign:
1987/88 league statistics: 6(-)-

Steve Hardwick had been in goal for Newcastle on the night they conceded nine at home to Sunderland. Not in the famous 9-1 win in 1908 but in 1979 in a League Cup tie which Sunderland won 7-6 on penalties after a 2-2 draw.

Earlier in the year he'd also been the Magpies goalie beaten by Gary Rowell's legendary hat-trick. In all he kept 25 clean sheets in 92 league games for the Tynesiders but didn't relish the pressure of playing in the north-east.

Brought in on loan from Oxford United, Hardwick played in the opening six league games of the season, plus a couple of Wear–Tees derbies in the Littlewoods (League) Cup. Although he kept three clean sheets and did well, he elected not to continue on Wearside when given the opportunity. Instead, he returned to Oxford where he made four top-flight appearances later in the season, but having been cup-tied with Sunderland couldn't be considered as the U's reached the League Cup semi-finals.

––––––

HARDYMAN, Paul
Date of birth: 11 March 1964
Place of birth: Portsmouth
Position: Left-back

Promotion campaign:
1989/90 league statistics: 42(-)7 Play-offs 1(-)-

A team-mate of Kevin Ball at Portsmouth, Hardyman moved from Fratton Park to Roker a year ahead of Bally and proved to be an effective left-back. With the help of four penalties his seven goals in his promotion season put the defender within two goals of being second-top league scorer, but it was a penalty that cost him his place at Wembley. Sent off in the aftermath of having his spot kick saved in the semi-final against Newcastle, it proved to be doubly costly for Paul who two years later was devastated to only be a sub at Wembley in the FA Cup Final, having started every other match of the cup run.

HARTLEY, Peter

Date of birth: 3 April 1988
Place of birth: Hartlepool
Position: Centre-back

Promotion campaign:
2006/07 league statistics: -(1)-

A New Year's Day appearance as a late sub in a win at Leicester proved to be academy product Peter Hartley's solitary first-team game for Sunderland. He went on to have a lengthy career elsewhere, particularly at his home-town club where he totalled 181 games, once scoring alongside James Poole as Hartley and Poole scored for Hartlepool.

In 2021 Peter was playing in India, for Jamshedpur.

―――

HARVEY, Martin

Date of birth: 19 September 1941
Place of birth: Belfast
Position: Midfielder

Promotion campaign:
1963/64 league statistics: 32 0

Harvey was so good Sunderland felt able to let Stan Anderson go. At international level Martin replaced the legendary Danny Blanchflower and went on to set a record that still stands in 2021, as Sunderland's most-capped player for any of the four home nations – with 34 caps for Northern Ireland. A skilful player whose timing in the tackle was exceptional, Harvey was consistently reliable whether at half-back or full-back. After ten games of the promotion season Martin came in to replace Anderson. Once in the side he kept his place for the rest of the campaign and went on to total 358 games for the club.

HAUSER, Thomas

Date of birth: 10 April 1965
Place of birth: Schopfheim, Germany
Position: Centre-forward

Promotion campaign:
1989/90 league statistics: 6(12)6 Play-offs -(1)-

Rather like Lilian Laslandes and Tore André Flo were meant to replace Niall Quinn as Kevin Phillips's partner, so Thomas Hauser was intended to take over from veteran Eric Gates alongside Marco Gabbiadini. Hauser, though, was a totally different player to schemer Gates, being more of a target man. He did, however, score the last goal of the 80s and the first of the 90s and never gave less than 100 per cent. Used as a sub in the play-off final, three decades after the game and by then living in Switzerland, Hauser was still one of those players passionate about Sunderland.

———

HAWKE, Warren

Date of birth: 20 March 1970
Place of birth: Durham
Position: Forward

Promotion campaign:
1989/90 league statistics: 1(7)1 Play-offs 1(-)-

Warren Hawke only ever started ten games for Sunderland and came on as sub 19 times, but he got a start in the play-off semi-final second leg at Newcastle and made a Wembley appearance in the FA Cup Final two years later as a sub. An elegant and smooth-moving footballer with a clever football brain, it was Hawke who fed the ball to the G-force when they combined for Gabbiadini to score in the play-off at St James'.

HAWLEY, John

Date of birth: 8 May 1954
Place of birth: Patrington, East Yorkshire
Position: Forward

Promotion campaign:
1979/80 league statistics: 9(-)4

Signed for a club-record-equalling £200,000, centre-forward John Hawley was known to manager Ken Knighton from their time at Hull City. In the early days of his career Hawley played as an amateur as he had interests in his family's antiques business.

Marking his league debut with a hat-trick at home to Charlton, John added another goal in the next home game against QPR but missed most of the season through injury. He did, however, return for the crucial final game against West Ham, his first outing since the first week of January.

Once promoted, Hawley scored the opening goal of the campaign in a win over Everton and followed that up with a hat-trick at Manchester City, as he fired Sunderland to the top of the embryonic top-flight table. After another long spell out he returned with a famous goal from fully 40 yards against Arsenal. When he played Hawley was dangerous, but in his time at Sunderland he didn't play enough.

——

HEATHCOTE, Mickey

Date of birth: 10 September 1965
Place of birth: Kelloe, Co. Durham
Position: Defender

Promotion campaigns:
1987/88 league statistics: -(1)-
1989/90 league statistics: 6(4)- Play-offs -(-)-

A debutant, as sub, for fellow debutant Richard Ord on the night the Shrimpers of Southend found their net bulging at Roker, this proved to be Heathcote's only appearance of the 1987/88 campaign.

Two seasons later he reached double figures, including substitute appearances. For the play-off semi-final against Newcastle the club requested he was pictured on the programme cover in recognition of his efforts in a season where he had struggled with injury. It was the only time in over three decades of putting the programme together that I received such a request.

———

HENDERSON, Mick
Date of birth: 31 March 1956
Place of birth: Gosforth
Position: Defender

Promotion campaign:
1975/76 league statistics: 11(2)1

A teenager when he debuted during his promotion season in a big win at York, Mick Henderson was a versatile player. Two-footed, he debuted at left-back and made almost all of his appearances in his breakthrough season on the left-hand side, although he was at his best on the right. A Boxing Day scorer against Hull City when he was operating on the left of midfield, Mick's promotion season strike was one of only two he managed in a total of 95 appearances for the club.

———

HERD, George
Date of birth: 6 May 1936
Place of birth: Glasgow
Position: Inside-forward

Promotion campaign:
1963/64 league statistics: 39 13

A Scotland international who cost a club record £42,500 when bought from Clyde in 1961, George Herd was a skilful and creative inside-forward. He also possessed endless energy. When man-marked Herd's tactic was to run his marker into the ground before taking advantage when the opponent tired. Remember that in his promotion campaign substitutes were yet to be introduced to the game. Injured for three games in September, George played every other match and was third-top scorer. One of his goals was the winner in the home derby with Newcastle, while George also found the back of the net in the game where promotion was secured against Charlton Athletic.

———

HESFORD, Iain

Date of birth: 4 March 1960
Place of birth: Ndola, Zambia
Position: Goalkeeper

Promotion campaign:
1987/88 league statistics: 39(-)-

Having endured a torrid time as Sunderland were relegated in 1987 Iain Hesford lost his place to on-loan Steve Hardwick at the start of the promotion season, but when ex-Newcastle keeper Hardwick decided he didn't want to face the pressure of playing permanently in the north-east again Hesford was summoned. His return came at Gillingham who were not only the side who had relegated Sunderland in the previous season's play-offs, but a side so in form they had won their previous two home games 8-1 and 10-0. Hesford rose to the occasion, keeping a clean sheet, and carried on his redemption with an outstanding season that saw him miss just one of the last 40 games and finish as runner-up to Eric Gates as Player of the Year. He passed away in 2014.

———

HINDMARCH, Rob

Date of birth: 27 April 1961
Place of birth: Stannington
Position: Defender

Promotion campaign:
1979/80 league statistics: 21(-)-

Rob Hindmarch was a colossus of a central defender: big, powerful and commanding. A debutant at 16 and captain at 19, Hindmarch was 18 when the promotion season commenced. He came into the side for a run of six games, including a cup tie, in the autumn and then returned in February. From that point Rob kept his place to the end of the season, doing so well that he partnered Jeff Clarke at centre-back, allowing Shaun Elliott to be utilised in midfield.

Capped by England at youth level, Hindmarch went on to enjoy back-to-back promotions as skipper of Derby County, but sadly lost his life to motor neurone disease. He passed away in Philadelphia, USA in 2002 when he was just 41.

―――

HINNIGHAN, Joe
Date of birth: 3 December 1955
Place of birth: Liverpool
Position: Defender

Promotion campaign:
1979/80 league statistics: 14(-)-

Signed in February 1980, Joe Hinnigan became Sunderland's promotion mascot. Having lost the last match before his debut, Sunderland were unbeaten in the last 14 games as Hinnigan slotted into the left-back slot. The Liverpudlian had arrived for £135,000, a record fee for a Fourth Division player, as he joined from Wigan Athletic. Earlier in the season he had scored six goals from left-back for the Latics, including three in two games against Darlington and an FA Cup goal against Northwich Victoria, before helping Wigan to a shock win at Chelsea.

―――

HOLDEN, Mel
Date of birth: 25 August 1954
Place of birth: Dundee
Position: Forward

Promotion campaign:
1975/76 league statistics: 31(5)12

Mel Holden was signed as a 20-year-old at the end of the 1974/75 season in which he had caught the eye when helping Third Division Preston knock Sunderland out of the League Cup. With North End he had been part of a three-pronged attack with future England international Tony Morley and legendary player-manager Bobby Charlton.

During the promotion season Mel finished just one goal behind top scorer Pop Robson, for whom he played the role of target man. He evidently impressed Bob Stokoe, who later signed him for a second time when he was with Blackpool. Sadly, Holden passed away at the young age of just 26 after suffering from motor neurone disease.

———

HOLLOWAY, Darren

Date of birth: 3 October 1977
Place of birth: Bishop Auckland
Position: Defender

Promotion campaign:
1998/99 league statistics: 1(5)-

Darren Holloway had done so well in the season before the 105-point campaign that he had earned international recognition for England at Under-21 level, but a back injury ruined his hopes of playing a major part in the promotion campaign. His handful of games all came from the end of February onwards. He was eventually sold to Wimbledon for more than £1m, going on to top a century of appearances for the Dons.

———

HOWEY, Lee

Date of birth: 1 April 1969
Place of birth: Sunderland
Position: Centre-forward/centre-half

Promotion campaign:
1995/96 league statistics: 17(10)3

Massively Violent and Decidedly Average, according to the title of his biography, Lee Howey was named on the team sheet for all but five of the 46 games as promotion was won in 1995/96, albeit he was often left on the bench. First and foremost a striker, he was sometimes called upon to operate in defence. Two of Lee's promotion season goals were winners against Barnsley and West Brom, with the third helping to earn a point at Portsmouth.

———

HUGHES, Billy

Date of birth: 30 December 1948
Place of birth: Coatbridge
Position: Forward

Promotion campaign:
1975/76 league statistics: 14(3)6

Billy was a great player for Sunderland but was on the fringe of the side in his promotion campaign in what was his penultimate season with the club. Inducted into the SAFC Hall of Fame at the second such dinner in 2020, Billy deserved more than the solitary cap he won with Scotland.

Top scorer for Sunderland during the FA Cup-winning season of 1972/73, his haul then included the winner in the semi-final and two in the replay win over Manchester City that was voted the greatest game ever staged at Roker Park. It was also Billy's corner that produced the only goal of the final. During the promotion season Billy scored in four home wins, including hitting the final goal of the term on the day the trophy was secured against Portsmouth.

———

HUGHES, Ian

Date of birth: 24 August 1961
Place of birth: Sunderland
Position: Midfielder

Promotion campaign:
1979/80 league statistics: 1(-)-

Ian Hughes played just one senior competitive game for his home-town club. Turning out at Swansea in November 1979, he saw his side take a first-minute lead only to succumb 3-1 and never played again, although a couple of games later he was an unused sub for a home win over Bristol Rovers.

Three days before his debut in South Wales Ian did get to play first-team football at Roker Park. He came on as a half-time substitute in the club's 1979 centenary game against an England XI.

He later had a season with Barnsley in 1981/82 without making a league appearance before returning to Sunderland, only for an injury to end his playing days before he could force his way back into the side. Hughes moved on to the coaching staff before scouting for West Ham.

——

HURLEY, Charlie
Date of birth: 4 October 1936
Place of birth: Cork
Position: Defender

Promotion campaign:
1963/64 league statistics: 41 5

Voted Sunderland's Player of the Century in the club's centenary year in 1979, Hurley was renowned as 'The greatest centre-half the world has ever seen'. A composed colossus, 'King' Charlie captained the 1964 promotion winners when he was runner-up to FA Cup-winning captain Bobby Moore as Footballer of the Year. Capped 40 times by the Republic of Ireland, Hurley was inducted into the Sunderland Hall of Fame at the inaugural dinner in 2019 and had an autobiography published in 2008. One of only two home defeats in the promotion season came against Southampton in the only game Hurley missed. Renowned as the first centre-half to go forward for corner kicks, Charlie scored five goals during the season plus a couple of others during the cup run.

HYSÉN, Tobias

Date of birth: 9 March 1982
Place of birth: Gothenburg, Sweden
Position: Midfielder/winger

Promotion campaign:
2006/07 league statistics: 15(11)4

Toby Hysén was a Sweden international signed for a sizeable £1.7m fee in the short period when Niall Quinn managed the team. He debuted in Niall's last game as manager and after sitting out the first couple of games under Roy Keane came off the bench in the new gaffer's first home game to score the first Stadium of Light goal as the 'Roy-volution' got going.

Coming from a family of footballers, Toby was a player of pedigree who spent much of the season alternating with Ross Wallace on the left flank. He contributed three further goals in victories but uncharacteristically blotted his copybook when he was one of the players left behind by the manager when late for the bus to Barnsley.

Before and after his spell at Sunderland Toby was a league and cup winner in his home country with Djurgarden and Gothenburg.

INGHAM, Michael

Date of birth: 7 September 1980
Place of birth: Preston
Position: Goalkeeper

Promotion campaign:
2004/05 league statistics: 1(1)-

With the Lads on the brink of promotion, goalkeeper Ingham came off the bench for the injured Thomas Myhre against Reading. That game was lost at the Stadium of Light and when Michael was judged to be at fault for a goal as points were dropped a few days later at Ipswich, he swiftly found himself back on the bench. He was dropped in favour of teenager Ben Alnwick as promotion was secured in the following match. Michael played only two other games for Sunderland but went on to enjoy success with York, for whom he played over 300 times. He also ended his career with three full international caps for Northern Ireland.

_____

IRWIN, Cec
Date of birth: 8 April 1942
Place of birth: Ellington
Position: Defender

Promotion campaign:
1963/64 league statistics: 39 -

Sunderland's youngest-ever player when he debuted as a 16-year-old in 1958, right-back Irwin began to establish himself in 1961 and remained part of the team until 1971 when he made his 352nd appearance. During the first promotion season Cec played every game until March, when he was ruled out for three matches before returning for the run-in. Firmly established as first choice, Cec also played in all seven of the promotion campaign's cup games. A long-striding full-back, the sight of Cec storming forward to deliver crosses was a familiar part of the game for a team who liked to attack. A lifelong Sunderland supporter, Cec has continued to regularly attend home games as a member of the Former Players' Association.

_____

JOHN, Stern
Date of birth: 30 October 1976
Place of birth: Tunapuna, Trinidad
Position: Centre-forward

Promotion campaign:
2006/07 league statistics: 10(5)4

Stern John scored against Sunderland on the first day of the promotion season for Coventry. In 2003 his showboating when a Birmingham player had seen Marcus Stewart exact revenge with a resultant red card on a day relegation was mathematically confirmed.

Roy Keane added Stern to the red and white ranks in the January transfer window as he looked to boost his side's firepower. Debuting against Coventry, who he had just left, he scored his first two goals in his second home game against Southend. He went on to notch a winner at West Brom and also score in a home win over Hull. As well as winning promotion with Sunderland, Stern had success in the 2002 play-offs with Birmingham. His 70 international goals in 115 games included strikes against Scotland and Wales.

———

JOHNSON, Simon

Date of birth: 9 March 1983
Place of birth: West Bromwich
Position: Forward

Promotion campaign:
2004/05 league statistics: 1(4)-

Simon Johnson came to Sunderland for the third of five loans he had from his first club Leeds. After four appearances as sub, he was given a start in a hard-fought home win over Millwall but was substituted and not called upon again.

He went on to play for Darlington and Hereford, being a promotion winner with the Bulls in 2008, mainly playing as a winger. After a brief spell with Bury, he dropped into non-league when he was only 26, never to return to the Football League.

———

JOHNSTON, Allan

Date of birth: 14 December 1973
Place of birth: Glasgow
Position: Winger

Promotion campaign:
1998/99 league statistics: 40(-)7

'Magic' Johnston was a right-footer playing on the left wing. His combination with left-back Mickey Gray was one of several brilliant partnerships in the team that swept to the title in the most convincing fashion in 1999. The jinkiest of jinky wingers, Johnston was a nightmare to defend against. With the energetic Gray overlapping, he always had the option of playing his team-mate in. With Gray pulling away one of his markers, Allan's trademark was to drop his shoulder, cut inside and either find Niall Quinn or Kevin Phillips, with the alternative of curling the ball into the top corner of the net.

Capped with Scotland for the first time during the promotion season, Johnston marked his fifth and sixth internationals with his first Scotland goals in the month after the league season ended. Having scored the last league goal at Roker Park against Everton in the Premier League, very sadly he would not go on to grace the Premier League again with Sunderland after Peter Reid sidelined him as he entered the final season of his contract.

———

KAVANAGH, Graham

Date of birth: 2 December 1973
Place of birth: Dublin
Position: Midfield

Promotion campaign:
2006/07 league statistics: 10(4)1

Graham Kavanagh had often excelled against Sunderland, so when Roy Keane made his fellow Republic of Ireland international one of his deadline day signings after taking over, his acquisition was one which showed the club meant business. A driving force in the centre of the park, 'Kav' scored a peach of a goal at Leeds in his and the new gaffer's second game, but after just two more appearances was injured. He returned at Halloween but by Christmas had played his final game of the term as injury struck again. The following season he played just once, in the FA Cup, but sadly Graham's time on Wearside was frustratingly short.

KAY, JOHN

Date of birth: 29 January 1964
Place of birth: Great Lumley
Position: Defender

Promotion campaigns:
1987/88 league statistics: 46(-)-
1989/90 league statistics: 31(1)- Play-offs 3(-)-

John returned to his native north-east after starting his career in the capital with Arsenal and Wimbledon. He became a cult hero at Roker Park as a result of his phenomenal determination and liking for a tough tackle in the days when you could challenge with great physicality. Future Sunderland manager Howard Wilkinson once complained one of his players looked like he'd been run over by a tractor after being tackled by John.

Slotting straight into the side, Kay played in every league game as he helped Denis Smith's side to promotion. Although the only games he missed in his first promotion season were a Sherpa Van Trophy game and an FA Cup defeat at Scunthorpe, he was unlucky to miss the 1992 FA Cup Final through injury. In 1993 his 199th and final league game for the club saw John managing a joke even after he broke his leg. As he was stretchered off Kay famously sat up and pretended to row the stretcher as if it was a boat.

KELLY, David

Date of birth: 25 November 1965
Place of birth: Birmingham
Position: Striker

Promotion campaign:
1995/96 league statistics: 9(1)2

David 'Ned' Kelly became Sunderland's first £1m player almost by default. Bought from Wolves for an initial £900,000, the extra £100,000 that made the deal a seven-figure one came about as a result of Sunderland winning promotion. However, due to injury Kelly had hardly played, not featuring at all after mid-January. Things had begun well with goals in his second and third games as he got his eye in, but he was never able to capture the form that had seen him score 28 times in a promotion season as he had in 1992/93 for Kevin Keegan's Newcastle. David had also won promotion with his first club Walsall in 1988 when he scored a hat-trick in the play-off final replay against Bristol City, who had former Sunderland youth-teamer Keith Waugh in goal.

A Republic of Ireland international, David scored nine times in winning his 26 full caps.

———

KERR, Andy

Date of birth: 29 June 1931
Place of birth: Lugar
Position: Forward

Promotion campaign:
1963/64 league statistics: 10 3

No relation to Bobby Kerr, Andy Kerr scored the first goal of the first-ever promotion season and played in the opening nine games as centre-forward, before losing his place to Nick Sharkey. He returned in November as stand-in centre-half for Charlie Hurley in a home defeat to Southampton, before moving on to Aberdeen the following April.

———

KERR, Bobby

Date of birth: 16 November 1947
Place of birth: Alexandria
Position: Midfield

Promotion campaign:
1975/76 league statistics: 40(-)7

Bobby entered Sunderland folklore as the captain of the FA Cup winners in 1973. He was a midfielder who never stopped running.

A creative player who chipped in with plenty of goals, including seven in his promotion season, Kerr had burst on to the scene as a goalscoring sensation. Starting with the winner on his debut against Manchester City on New Year's Eve going into 1967, the teenager netted seven in his first 11 games – including a brace against Newcastle – before he broke his leg. That injury came in a cup tie against Leeds, who six years later he would face at Wembley in the cup final. Bobby was inducted into the club's Hall of Fame at its inaugural dinner in 2019.

––––

KUBICKI, Dariusz

Date of birth: 6 June 1963
Place of birth: Kożuchów, Poland
Position: Right-back

Promotion campaign:
1995/96 league statistics: 46(-)-

One of two ever-presents (with Mickey Gray) in his promotion season, Poland international Kubicki was one of the most consistent players seen at Sunderland in recent decades. Ultra-dependable, Dariusz would never be a match-winner but he would never be a match-loser either. Mistakes from him were exceptionally rare; he was invariably composed and a quality player whose attitude was superb. On one occasion when badly injured he wouldn't let the physio take his boot off at half-time because he knew that with swelling he would never get it back on again and neither did he want to come off. Contrast that with some of the more recent players whose willingness to play was highly questionable.

Dariusz went on to have an extensive managerial career, mainly in his home country, while his son Patryk was with Sunderland as a very young player before going on to play as a midfielder with clubs in Poland and Russia.

Captain Charlie Hurley is chaired aloft on the lap of honour in 1964. With Hurley from left to right: Nick Sharkey, George Mulhall, Johnny Crossan, Cecil Irwin, Jimmy McNab, Len Ashurst, Jim Montgomery, Brian Usher and George Herd.

Bryan 'Pop' Robson (shirtless) celebrates with Billy Hughes after the second division title was sealed against Portsmouth on 24 April 1976.

Argentinian midfielder Claudio Marangoni became Sunderland's second record breaking signing during the 1979/80 promotion season.

The 1980 promotion winning team. The silverware is the Daily Express 5-a-side trophy. Sunderland squad for the 1980-81 season. (Back l-r) Joe Bolton, Gordon Chisholm, Claudio Marangoni, Chris Turner, Rob Hindmarch, Kevin Arnott and Steve Whitworth. (Middle row l-r) Jimmy Greenhaigh (chief Scout), Jack Watson (scout), Shaun Elliott, Sam Allardyce, Jeff Clarke, John Hawley, Joe Hinnigan, Alan Brown, Barry Dunn, Bryan Robson, John Watters (physio) and Charlie Ferguson (youth development officer). (Front row l-r) Mick Docherty (coach), Mick Buckley, Stan Cummins, Ken Knighton (manager), Frank Clark (assistant manager), John Cooke, Gary Rowell and Peter Eustace (coach).

Richard Ord pictured on his debut as Sunderland won 7-0 against Southend United on 3 November 1987.

Marco Gabbiadini and Eric Gates in action in the league draw at Newcastle on 4 February 1990.

Craig Russell flies the flag with the Division One trophy in 1996.

Kevin Phillips made a scoring comeback at QPR on 9 January 1999.

Allan 'Magic' Johnston with the Division One trophy at the climax of the '105-points' 1998/99 campaign.

Stephen Elliott celebrates scoring the only game of the game at Crewe on 12 March 2005 with skipper Dean Whitehead.

Mick McCarthy kisses the trophy after the Championship was won in 2005.

Danny Collins celebrates Grant Leadbitter's winner at QPR on 28 November 2006.

The players celebrate clinching the Championship with a 5-0 win at Luton on 6 May 2007. Left to right: Carlos Edwards, Stern John, Nyron Nosworthy, Danny Collins, Darren Ward, Danny Simpson, Anthony Stokes, Stephen Wright, David Connolly, Marton Fulop and Ross Wallace.

The squad pose with the Championship trophy in 2007 after it was presented at Seaham Hall.

KYLE, Kevin

Date of birth: 7 June 1981
Place of birth: Stranraer
Position: Centre-forward

Promotion campaigns:
2004/05 league statistics: 5(1)-
2006/07 league statistics: -(2)-

Kevin Kyle barely played in the promotion campaigns he featured in but in total played over 100 times for the club, where in his best season he scored 16 times in 2003/04, including in both legs of a play-off with Crystal Palace. Never the silkiest of players, 'Kyler' was all arms and legs, at times a bit ungainly, but never ever a player who gave less than 100 per cent. Centre-halves definitely knew they had been in a game with him, with the result that whoever his strike partner was, they had a bit more space as Kevin worked so hard.

The north-east Young Player of the Year in 2004, he won ten caps for Scotland and as Rangers worked their way through the leagues after their demotion, he helped them to promotion as Third Division champions in 2012/13 when he scored three times in eight league games.

_____

LAWRENCE, Liam

Date of birth: 14 December 1981
Place of birth: Worksop
Position: Midfield

Promotion campaigns:
2004/05 league statistics: 20(12)6
2006/07 league statistics: 10(2)-

Liam Lawrence's three eventful seasons at Sunderland brought two promotions either side of a relegation. Stepping up from Mansfield, 'Lennie' showed plenty of creative spirit, could deliver telling crosses and chipped in with some terrific goals, including a cracker at Cardiff and a couple in a home win over Wolves in the first of his promotion seasons.

Lawrence was something of a promotion specialist. Having been promoted with the Stags before coming to Sunderland, he went on to win further promotions with Stoke, Shrewsbury and twice with Bristol Rovers. In his first year after leaving Sunderland he was the Championship Player of the Season and Potters Player of the Year as he went up with Stoke.

———

LEADBITTER, Grant

Date of birth: 7 January 1986
Place of birth: Fence Houses, Co. Durham
Position: Midfield

Promotion campaign:
2006/07 league statistics: 24(20)7

Grant first appeared for Sunderland as a sub in a League Cup meeting with Huddersfield in September 2003, and sat on the bench in the home game with West Ham during the 2004/05 promotion season when he played in the League Cup but not in the league. Having started to break through in the Premier League in 2005/06, the 2006/07 promotion campaign was Leadbitter's first as a regular. He played in all but two games, a little over half of his appearances being in the starting line-up. He was named on the team sheet in every league fixture, remaining as an unused sub just twice.

A quality player who read the game expertly from a young age, Leadbitter played international football from schoolboy level to Under-21s. He played over 100 games for Ipswich and more than 200 for Middlesbrough, before reportedly taking a pay cut to come back to his home club to complete his career. A promotion winner with Boro in 2016, Grant made three appearances at Wembley in his second spell at Sunderland, playing in the 2019 League One play-off final and the EFL Trophy Finals of 2019 and 2021, winning on the second occasion after losing the earlier one on penalties.

LEE, Bob

Date of birth: 2 February 1953
Place of birth: Melton Mowbray
Position: Forward
Promotion campaign:
1979/80 league statistics: 7(-)1

Sunderland's first £200,000 signing when Bob Stokoe bought him in 1976, Lee's last appearances for the club came in the early part of the promotion season, before he left for Bristol Rovers at the end of the campaign. His final goal for the Lads came back at his former club Leicester City.

Tanned and toned, Lee looked like a comic-book image of a centre-forward. Initially coming into a struggling side for a record fee, expectation weighed heavily upon him and generally it was perceived that he failed to deliver as much as hoped for. However, his overall total of 33 goals in 114 starts plus eight substitute appearances are hardly the figures of a failure.

———

LEMON, Paul

Date of birth: 3 June 1966
Place of birth: Middlesbrough
Position: Midfielder/forward
Promotion campaign:
1987/88 league statistics: 35(6)9

Never the darling of the crowd, Paul Lemon was a regular in the 1987/88 promotion side, scoring nine league goals and a dozen in total. Only the front two of Gates and Gabbiadini and penalty king MacPhail scored more. Lemon did this despite playing out of position on the right of midfield rather than in his preferred position of striker, a role he did well in when developing as a youth but very rarely played at first-team level.

Commonly known as 'Jack' after the Hollywood star Jack Lemmon, Paul provided plenty of energy to the team. Aged 21 throughout the promotion season, he did a lot of unselfish running and was never found wanting in terms of effort. In the 1989/90 promotion season Lemon was an unused sub in home games with Ipswich and Bournemouth but played in a couple of cup games.

_____

LONGHORN, Dennis

Date of birth: 12 September 1950
Place of birth: Southampton
Position: Midfield

Promotion campaign:
1975/76 league statistics: 6(2)1

A long-striding midfielder, Dennis Longhorn spent much of his time at Sunderland on the fringe of the first team. This was certainly the case in 1975/76 when he was limited to a handful of appearances. He scored the winner against Chelsea on the opening day of the season but lost his place after a 3-0 defeat at Bristol City next time out. Those were the only back-to-back starts he had in the league, although he was called upon from time to time and started the FA Cup quarter-final with Crystal Palace.

_____

LYNCH, Mark

Date of birth: 2 September 1981
Place of birth: Manchester
Position: Right-back

Promotion campaign:
2004/05 league statistics: 5(6)-

Mark Lynch had played in a Champions League game for Manchester United against Deportivo La Coruña 16 months before joining Sunderland on a free transfer. It was Lynch's only appearance for the Red Devils, where he had come through the ranks. While he had acquired experience on loan with St Johnstone, there were to be only 13 games for Sunderland, all of which came in the 2004/05 Coca-

Cola Championship-winning season. Of those appearances 11 came in the league campaign. Almost all of these came in the first half of the season when he was very much part of the first-team scene, often at least being on the bench even if unused.

The simple truth of the matter, however, was that Lynch never really looked the part and after Christmas featured just twice, one of those as an unused sub. Given a free transfer at the end of the season he went on to play for five other clubs, but never reached a half century of appearances for anyone.

———

MacPHAIL, John
Date of birth: 7 December 1955
Place of birth: Dundee
Position: Defender

Promotion campaigns:
1987/88 league statistics: 46(-)16
1989/90 league statistics: 38(-)2 Play-offs 3(-)-

Manager Denis Smith – a rugged centre-half in his own playing days – knew exactly what he was getting when he signed John MacPhail for Sunderland's first-ever season in the Third Division. MacPhail had played for Smith at York City, being a mainstay of the Minstermen side who waltzed Division Four with 101 points in 1984.

At a cost of a meagre £23,000, the purchase of MacPhail from Bristol City combined with the signing of right-back John Kay gave Smith two battle-hardened defenders ready for the rigours of the level Sunderland were entering. Ever present in the promotion season, 'Monty' MacPhail was magnificent. A no-nonsense defender, he was also third-top scorer behind the G-force of Gates and Gabbiadini. The conversion of 11 out of 12 penalties contributed towards John scoring 16 goals, a club seasonal record for a defender. Two years later he remained a regular as the journey to the top flight was completed.

McCANN, Gavin

Date of birth: 10 January 1978
Place of birth: Blackpool
Position: Midfield

Promotion campaign:
1998/99 league statistics: 5(6)-

'He tackles and he passes, he hassles and harasses, he gets up people's asses, he's better than Roy Keane. Gavin McCann (click click), Gavin McCann (click click).' Sung to the tune of the *Addams Family* theme, the chant in midfielder McCann's honour summed him up perfectly. Plucked from Everton reserves for a bargain fee, McCann became one of Peter Reid's great signings. His promotion year was McCann's first season at the club, after which he spent four years in the Premier League with Sunderland, during which he was capped by England. Gavin's debut came in a 4-0 win at Sheffield United on the day the Blades' player-manager Steve Bruce decided to hang up his boots.

———

McCARTNEY, George

Date of birth: 29 April 1981
Place of birth: Belfast
Position: Left-back

Promotion campaign:
2004/05 league statistics: 35(1)-

Northern Ireland international George McCartney's left-flank partnership with Julio Arca was arguably the most exciting combination within the side who won the Championship in 2004/05. Youth team product McCartney was in his fifth season as a first teamer and was in top form as he defended with aplomb and supported the attack at every opportunity. The duo were similar in style to the Michael Gray–Allan Johnston pairing that were part of the previous promotion in 1998/99.

McCartney moved on to West Ham in 2006 and then re-signed in 2008, at the time becoming the most expensive signing to come through the Sunderland academy – only for the fee to have been paid by Sunderland! George went on to rejoin the Hammers after a couple of loans with Leeds. A class act, he was Sunderland's Player of the Year in his promotion season and also West Ham's as they were promoted via the play-offs in 2012. In 2004/05 at Sunderland he was also selected for the PFA Championship Team of the Year.

———

McGUIRE, Doug
Date of birth: 6 September 1967
Place of birth: Bathgate, Glasgow
Position: Midfielder

Promotion campaign:
1987/88 league statistics: 1(-)-

Doug McGuire's only game for Sunderland saw him substituted in a 2-1 defeat at York, where his replacement and fellow debutant Colin Pascoe scored Sunderland's goal. On loan from Celtic, McGuire later had an unsuccessful time at Coventry before returning north of the border, where in his time at Albion Rovers he set a Scottish League record by becoming the first man to score a hat-trick of penalties. He had started at Celtic where he created two goals on his debut to turn a game against Falkirk and later played against Borussia Dortmund in Europe, but in total only managed four games.

———

McNAB, Jim
Date of birth: 13 April 1940
Place of birth: Denny, Stirling
Position: Midfielder

Promotion campaign:
1963/64 league statistics: 37 2

A debutant on the same day as full-backs Cec Irwin and Len Ashurst in September 1958, the trio went on to total over 1,100 appearances for the club with 'Jimmy Mac' responsible for 323 of them. An important team player, McNab formed part of a supreme half-back line while simultaneously being the man right-wingers had to get past before they even came up against left-back Len Ashurst. Injury cost Jim a run of eight games in 1963/64, including the three-game cup epic with Manchester United. Belatedly, in May 1999 he became the first man to have a testimonial at the Stadium of Light. The first of the class of '64 to pass away, his captain Charlie Hurley delivered a heartfelt eulogy at 'Mac the Knife's' funeral in Sunderland.

———

MAKIN, Chris
Date of birth: 8 May 1973
Place of birth: Manchester
Position: Right-back

Promotion campaign:
1998/99 league statistics: 37(1)-

Born on the day Sunderland brought the cup home in 1973, Chris 'Shoot' Makin became a hugely popular player in his time on Wearside. He totalled approaching 150 games in four seasons, of which his promotion year was his second. Makin had played at Roker Park for England in a schoolboy international against Brazil during an earlier promotion season in 1988, but in 1998/99 played in what was a record-breaking campaign. His right-wing partnership with his great friend Nicky Summerbee was a highlight of a truly great side.

———

MALONE, Dick
Date of birth: 22 August 1947
Place of birth: Motherwell
Position: Defender

Promotion campaign:
1975/76 league statistics: 39(-)-

Right-back Dick Malone was an outstanding servant to the club and stayed in the city after his playing days, continuing to be a regular as a former player welcoming supporters in the corporate hospitality areas. In his playing days Malone was the epitome of a marauding full-back. Elegantly composed on the ball, he could appear ungainly on his trademark forward runs that earned him the nickname 'Tricky Dicky', but he was rarely dispossessed and earned cult hero status with the crowd.

A Scotland Under-23 international from his time with Ayr United, Dick later won another promotion at the tail end of his career with Queen of the South. However, without doubt Dick's greatest achievement was as a member of the legendary 1973 FA Cup winners.

――――

MARANGONI, Claudio
Date of birth: 17 November 1954
Place of birth: Rosario, Argentina
Position: Midfielder

Promotion campaign:
1979/80 league statistics: 16(-)3

Just a month after breaking the club transfer record to sign Stan Cummins, Ken Knighton did so again to acquire Argentinian Claudio Marangoni from San Lorenzo for £380,000. In due course only £230,000 was paid as he returned to South America after a year.

Back in Argentina Marangoni went on to become an international and won the continent's major honours with Independiente and Boca Juniors. At Sunderland, though, he mostly looked like a fish out of water. His style of play seemed alien to his team-mates and while other Argentinians had come into English football and excited supporters, such as Ossie Ardiles and Ricky Villa at Spurs and Alex Sabella at Sheffield United, Claudio paraded few of the silky skills fans hoped to see from a flair player.

――――

MARRIOTT, Andy
Date of birth: 11 October 1970
Place of birth: Sutton-in-Ashfield
Position: Goalkeeper

Promotion campaign:
1998/99 league statistics: 1(-)-

Andy Marriott had an even harder task than Michael Bridges and Danny Dichio in the 105-point promotion season. While Bridges and Dichio waited in the wings for a chance to replace Superkev and Quinny, Marriott had to wait for an opportunity to replace the Great Dane Tommy Sørensen. In the days of three subs being named Peter Reid preferred to go without a sub keeper, so Marriott didn't spend the season on the bench. When Sørensen had to go off in a game at eventual runners-up Bradford, Niall Quinn took over in goal with Marriott getting his chance in the next match at Grimsby, where he lived up to his undoubted pedigree by keeping a clean sheet.

_____

MELVILLE, Andy
Date of birth: 29 November 1968
Place of birth: Swansea
Position: Centre-back

Promotion campaigns:
1995/96 league statistics: 40(-)4
1998/99 league statistics: 44(-)2

A mainstay in two promotions that were built on a solid defence. Only 25 goals were conceded in the 40 games he played in 1995/96, with eight leaked in the other six games. Three years later only 28 were conceded as Andy played all but two games in a record-breaking campaign. A Wales international, Sunderland's defence was never at sea when Melville was oozing confidence. He went on to top over 700 league games with Sunderland, being the only club where he exceeded 200.

_____

MILLER, Liam
Date of birth: 13 February 1981
Place of birth: Ballincollig

Position: Midfielder

Promotion campaign:
2006/07 league statistics: 24(6)2

Liam Miller's death from pancreatic cancer in 2018, four days before what would have been his 37th birthday, brought an outpouring of grief for a player who was as popular in the dressing room as he was quiet in his public profile. One of Roy Keane's deadline day signings, the manager knew him from Manchester United where 19 of his 22 appearances for the Red Devils were made in Keane's final season at Old Trafford. The gaffer had also played alongside Liam for Ireland, while Miller's senior debut at his first club Celtic had been handed to him by Martin O'Neill.

An industrious and inventive schemer reminiscent of Mick Buckley from the 1979/80 promotion side, Miller's main moment came with a late winner against promotion rivals Derby at the Stadium of Light 11 days after his 26th birthday. No one could know then that there would not be many more birthdays for a player taken far too young.

––––––

MILLER, Tommy

Date of birth: 8 January 1979
Place of birth: Shotton Colliery
Position: Midfielder

Promotion campaign:
2006/07 league statistics: 3(1)-

Tommy Miller barely featured in the promotion campaign under Roy Keane. After starting the first three games of the season under Niall Quinn, seven months later he got one substitute appearance under Keane, at Barnsley on the day Keane had left three players behind for being late for the bus. In between those games, under Quinn and Keane he played against Sunderland while on loan to Preston.

In 2012 Tommy did win a promotion from League One with Huddersfield, although despite being a penalty expert he failed to score with the Terriers' first spot kick of the shoot-out. He later became caretaker manager of Swindon following the departure of Paolo Di Canio, and also managed Spennymoor.

_____

MITCHELL, Bobby
Date of birth: 4 January 1955
Place of birth: South Shields
Position: Midfield

Promotion campaign:
1975/76 league statistics: -(1)-

Bobby Mitchell was a stylish midfield creator who was unlucky not to play more for the club where he had come through the ranks. In total he only appeared three times for Sunderland. His only appearance of the promotion season came as a 79th-minute substitute for goalscorer Tom Finney in the Boxing Day victory over Hull City. It was to be Bobby's final match for the club, who he left at the end of the season to sign for Blackburn Rovers prior to playing for Bobby Kerr's brother George at Grimsby, Rotherham, Lincoln and Boston.

_____

MITCHINSON, Tommy
Date of birth: 24 February 1943
Place of birth: Sunderland
Position: Forward

Promotion campaign:
1963/64 league statistics: 1 -

Tommy Mitchinson stood in for Brian Usher in a 4-1 home win over Leyton Orient in November 1963. That was the solitary appearance he managed in the promotion season, although he played 21 games in total before moving on to Mansfield Town in January 1966. Later in his career he played over 50 games for Aston Villa.

MONCUR, Bob

Date of birth: 19 January 1945
Place of birth: Perth
Position: Defender

Promotion campaign:
1975/76 league statistics: 39(-)2

Bob Moncur did for Sunderland what Stan Anderson did for Newcastle. Stan was a Roker legend who skippered the Magpies to promotion as a veteran. Moncur had captained Newcastle to the Inter-Cities Fairs Cup in 1969 and came to Wearside at the age of 29 to steer the Lads into the top flight.

A superb defender who had captained Scotland, Moncur combined class on the ball with strength and know-how. During the promotion campaign he missed a mere three games and chipped in with a couple of goals, at Oxford and at home to Charlton.

MONTGOMERY, Jim

Date of birth: 9 October 1943
Place of birth: Sunderland
Position: Goalkeeper

Promotion campaigns:
1963/64 league statistics: 42 -
1975/76 league statistics: 38(-)-

Sunderland's record appearance maker, his 627 games being 169 more than anyone else, Monty was ever present in the club's first-ever promotion and again a regular in the second a dozen years later. In between he made the most famous save ever seen at Wembley Stadium in the 1973 FA Cup Final. Supporters of the era knew that double save against Leeds was nothing unusual for the Mighty Jim, it just came in the most high profile of games. *Magnificent Monty* was the title of his 1974 testimonial programme and Monty was magnificent week in, week out. In 2021 he was still a club ambassador with a suite at the Stadium of Light named in his honour. Jim was inducted into the club's Hall of Fame at the inaugural dinner in 2019. Monty conceded just 37 goals in his 42 games in the first promotion season, keeping 20 clean sheets including a sequence of six successive league shutouts. A dozen years later he played every game bar the first two and the last two, conceding 31 goals and keeping 16 clean sheets, which included a run of four games without being beaten. In total Jim's 189 clean sheets are 42 more than anyone else has ever managed.

___

MOORE, John

Date of birth: 1 October 1966
Place of birth: Consett
Position: Forward

Promotion campaign:
1987/88 league statistics: -(9)-

Young centre-forward John Moore featured strongly in the early part of the 1987/88 promotion season. Named as sub in 11 of the first 12 league games, he came on seven times but dropped down the pecking order following the signing of Marco Gabbiadini. From mid-October onwards he only got on the bench twice more in the league.

Moore had made his debut three seasons earlier in the top flight, his only league goal for the club being a winner at Coventry. He also scored twice in the third-tier promotion season, netting in Sherpa Van Trophy games against Scarborough and Rotherham.

___

MULHALL, George

Date of birth: 8 May 1936
Place of birth: Standburn, Stirling
Position: Winger

Promotion campaign:
1963/64 league statistics: 42 9

Left-winger who played in every game of the first promotion season, as did his inside-left partner Johnny Crossan. A Scotland international, rather than be intimidated by the rough-house tactics defenders were able to get away with in this era, Mulhall could dish it out as well as take it – and defenders weren't used to tough wingers. Brave and direct on the ball, George was unusually good in the air for a winger. He emphasised his ever-present record by also playing in all cup ties, getting on the mark at Manchester United in the FA Cup quarter-final. He helped to get the promotion season off to a bright start with three goals in the opening two games, while one of his most important earned a share of the spoils at rivals Leeds on Boxing Day.

———

MULLIN, John
Date of birth: 11 August 1975
Place of birth: Bury
Position: Forward

Promotion campaigns:
1995/96 league statistics: 5(5)1
1998/99 league statistics: 8(1)2

Forever famous as the player who scored the last-ever goal at Roker Park in the farewell match against Liverpool, John Mullin won promotion in the first and last of his four seasons at Sunderland. In between he had loans to Preston and Burnley but never managed more than ten league appearances in a season for Sunderland. In 1995/96 he scored in a win over Luton, while in 1998/99 he scored twice in three games in early-season wins over Tranmere at home and Ipswich away. From 2014 to 2018 he was an academy coach at Manchester City and as of 2021 was still scouting for Pep Guardiola's side.

———

MURPHY, Daryl
Date of birth: 15 March 1983
Place of birth: Waterford
Position: Striker

Promotion campaign:
2006/07 league statistics: 27(11)10

Daryl Murphy came into his own in 2014/15 when he was the Championship's top scorer with 27 goals as he helped Ipswich to the play-offs, albeit the Tractor Boys lost to their local rivals Norwich. That season he was not surprisingly Ipswich's Player of the Year as well as being included in the PFA Championship Team of the Year.

His promotions came not in East Anglia but in the north-east. In 2016/17 he scored six times in 18 league outings as Newcastle took the title, while at Sunderland a decade earlier his ten goals included the first goal of the campaign at Coventry and two in the season's final game as a 5-0 win at his old club Luton clinched the title.

____

MYHRE, Thomas
Date of birth: 16 October 1973
Place of birth: Sarpsborg, Norway
Position: Goalkeeper

Promotion campaign:
2004/05 league statistics: 31(-)-

Norway international Myhre was a high-calibre but injury-prone goalkeeper. At one point he was one of four international keepers on the books along with Thomas Sørensen, Jürgen Macho and Mart Poom of Denmark, Austria and Estonia, but in the promotion season Myhre became first choice in late October and played every league game until April, when he had to go off in a match against Reading. That led to a goalkeeping problem as promotion was secured, with Myhre's replacement Michael Ingham swiftly dropped for the untried teenager Ben Alnwick.

____

NELSON, Colin
Date of birth: 13 March 1938
Place of birth: East Boldon
Position: Defender

Promotion campaign:
1963/64 league statistics: 3 -

An ever-present in 1960/61, by the first promotion season Nelson had lost his place at right-back to Cec Irwin. He came into the side for three games in March, starting with the derby at Newcastle three days after the cup quarter-final second replay with Manchester United. In Colin's early years at Sunderland he was training to be a pharmacist, often playing after attending class on a Saturday morning, but by 1964 he was full-time.

NORMAN, Tony
Date of birth: 24 February 1958
Place of birth: Mancot, Flintshire
Position: Goalkeeper

Promotion campaign:
1989/90 league statistics: 28(-)- Play-offs 3(-)-

An exceptionally calm and reliable goalkeeper, Wales international Norman had excellent positional sense and handling. A schoolboy with Burnley, he came to prominence with Hull City, having a blinder against Sunderland shortly before the Wearsiders signed him for a record fee of £450,000 that included Iain Hesford and Billy Whitehurst moving in part-exchange.

A broken arm early in the promotion season ruled him out for a long chunk of the campaign but he still played in two-thirds of the league programme and all of the play-offs, having another blinder at Wembley in the final. Two years later he became the first Sunderland keeper to play twice at the national stadium when he played in the FA Cup Final.

NOSWORTHY, Nyron
Date of birth: 11 October 1980
Place of birth: Brixton, London

Position: Defender

Promotion campaign:
2006/07 league statistics: 27(2)-

Known as 'Nugsy', the free-transfer signing from Gillingham went on to reach cult hero status due to his tremendous commitment and the way he bonded with the crowd, something notably seen on the final day of his promotion-winning season at Luton in the title-winning celebrations. Brought to the club as a right-back, he produced his best form after Roy Keane partnered him with Jonny Evans in a new centre-back pairing that provided the platform for a 17-match unbeaten run that propelled the team to promotion.

_____

NYATANGA, Lewin

Date of birth: 18 August 1988
Place of birth: Burton upon Trent
Position: Defender

Promotion campaign:
2006/07 league statistics: 9(2)-

Nyatanga came in on loan from Derby where he had been the Rams' Young Player of the Year the previous season. From a mid-October match with Barnsley until a New Year's Day trip to Leicester he featured strongly, but found himself surplus to requirements once Jonny Evans came in on loan from Manchester United. Almost a decade later Nyatanga enjoyed a promotion with Barnsley via the League One play-offs.

_____

ORD, Richard

Date of birth: 3 March 1970
Place of birth: Murton
Position: Defender

Promotion campaigns:
1987/88 league statistics: 4(4)0

1989/90 league statistics: 6(1)1 Play-offs -(-)-
1995/96 league statistics: 41(1)1

A debutant as Sunderland slaughtered Southend 7-0, Dickie Ord went on to become a cult hero at the club, a record even being made in his honour and entitled, 'Who Needs Cantona When We've Got Dickie Ord?' This was also the title of his 2012 autobiography, which is essential reading. Able to play in central defence, left-back or in midfield, Ord was a combination of commanding and yet cultured play. Sadly, Dickie's career suffered from injury problems – something that started with a broken leg as a three-year-old when falling off a settee when celebrating Ian Porterfield's winner for Sunderland in the 1973 FA Cup Final!

_____

OSTER, John
Date of birth: 8 December 1978
Place of birth: Boston, Lincs
Position: Winger

Promotion campaign:
2004/05 league statistics: 6(3)-

All of John Oster's appearances in his Sunderland promotion season came in the first two months of a campaign in which he played for two other Championship clubs. Loaned to Leeds in November and December, he signed for Burnley in January having been released by Sunderland. In total that term he played 30 times in Sunderland's division. A Wales international, he played in a couple of FIFA World Cup qualifiers shortly before his departure from the Black Cats. The following season he topped that with 33 Championship games for Reading as they gained 106 points to break Sunderland's 1998/99 record.

_____

OWERS, Gary
Date of birth: 3 October 1968
Place of birth: Newcastle

Position: Midfielder

Promotion campaigns:
1987/88 league statistics: 37(-)4
1989/90 league statistics: 43(-)9 Play-offs 3(-)-

Gary Owers debuted on the opening day of Sunderland's first-ever third-tier campaign and proved to be a key man in the side that won two promotions in his first three seasons. Rather like Brian Usher in the 1963/64 promotion year, Owers was the young newcomer in the side and one who provided boundless long-striding energy.

Like Gordon Armstrong, Owers was Tyneside-born but red and white to the core. Many years later when managing Forest Green Rovers in a friendly against Sunderland and bringing himself on as a sub, he made his side wear their away kit at home rather than play against Sunderland in their then home kit of black and white stripes. Second-top scorer to Gabbiadini in 1990, Owers was a great servant to the club and went on to play in the 1992 FA Cup Final.

——

PASCOE, Colin
Date of birth: 9 April 1965
Place of birth: Bridgend
Position: Midfielder

Promotion campaigns:
1987/88 league statistics: 8(1)4
1989/90 league statistics: 32(1)1 Play-offs 1(-)-

Brought in from Swansea in a £70,000 transfer deadline day deal to bolster the 1987/88 promotion campaign, Pascoe hit the ground running with a debut goal off the bench and scored three more times in the remaining eight games, starting them all.

Two years later the Wales international was a regular as promotion was won to the top flight. Although injured in the run-in to the end of the season, he recovered to play in the play-off final against Swindon at Wembley.

PHILLIPS, Kevin

Date of birth: 25 July 1973
Place of birth: Hitchin
Position: Striker

Promotion campaign:
1998/99 league statistics: 26(-)23

Sunderland's record post-war goalscorer, Superkev missed much of his promotion season due to an injury picked up in a League Cup tie with Chester, otherwise goodness knows if even more than 105 points would have been accrued. As it was Phillips smashed 23 in 26 games, including a stunning volley at QPR as he announced his comeback. The previous season he had broken Brian Clough's post-war seasonal record with 35 goals, while the following term he became the first Englishman to win the European Golden Shoe with 30 goals in 36 Premier League games. Phillips's form saw him make his England debut shortly before the end of his promotion season. In 2020 Superkev was inducted into the SAFC Hall of Fame.

––––

PIPER, Matt

Date of birth: 29 September 1981
Place of birth: Leicester
Position: Winger

Promotion campaign:
2004/05 league statistics: 1(1)-

Injury-raddled Matt Piper's pair of promotion season games came at the turn of the year against Preston and Gillingham. They would be his last league appearances for the club, although he did appear once in the League Cup the following season. Highly promising as a speed merchant when bought from his home team Leicester – for whom he had scored the last goal at their old Filbert Street ground – Matt's career was devastated by injury. His 2020 biography *Out of the Darkness* documented his fall from grace from Premier League footballer to an attempted suicide, but thankfully Matt got his life successfully back on track.

POOM, Mart

Date of birth: 3 February 1972
Place of birth: Tallinn, Estonia
Position: Goalkeeper

Promotion campaign:
2004/05 league statistics: 11(-)-

Renowned as a phenomenal trainer and model professional, Mart Poom was an excellent goalkeeper who was famed for the sensationally dramatic goal he scored against his former club Derby in 2003.

The 2004/05 promotion season saw Mart play 11 of the opening 14 league games, keeping five clean sheets only for injury to derail his season. Capped 120 times by his country, 'The Poominator' was Estonian Footballer of the Year six times.

___

PORTERFIELD, Ian

Date of birth: 11 February 1946
Place of birth: Dunfermline
Position: Midfielder

Promotion campaign:
1975/76 league statistics: 20(2)1

Immortalised as the scorer of the only goal of the 1973 FA Cup Final, Ian Porterfield was a cultured creator of goals. 'Porter' always had time on the ball and would remain unhurried in even the most frenetic of games.

The promotion season Porterfield played in was his last at Sunderland. He later went on loan to Reading – managed by Charlie Hurley – in November 1976. Ian had been severely injured in a car crash a day after one of his finest performances for the club in a 4-1 victory over Portsmouth in December 1974. His final match for Sunderland was at Chelsea, who he went on to manage, while his last game at home against Oxford ended with the appropriate scoreline of 1-0, with Porterfield the scorer. As a manager he led Rotherham United and Sheffield United to promotion from the

Third Division in 1981 and 1984, having also lifted the Blades out of Division Four in 1982. He also had another FA Cup win as a manager – in South Korea with Busan I'Park in 2004. The story of Ian's cup wins was told in *The Impossible Dream* (1973) and *Who Ate All the Squid?* (2020).

_____

PROCTOR, Mark
Date of birth: 30 January 1961
Place of birth: Middlesbrough
Position: Midfielder

Promotion campaign:
1987/88 league statistics: 4(-)-

The final four of Mark Proctor's 138 Sunderland appearances were the first four fixtures of his promotion-winning season. That Sunderland were in the Third Division in the first place was partly down to Proctor, though that basic statement is undeniably harsh. A talented midfield creator who had represented England at Under-21 level, 'Proc' had scored twice – including a penalty – in the first leg of the relegation play-off at Gillingham but fluffed a spot kick in the second leg when Sunderland eventually lost on away goals. He had also failed from the spot in the final regular league game against Barnsley, which resulted in Sunderland being condemned to the play-offs.

At least Proctor had the bottle to take the penalties. His character and ability were not in question and soon after dropping into the third tier a club-record-equalling sale fee of £275,000 was accepted from top-flight Sheffield Wednesday.

_____

QUINN, Niall
Date of birth: 6 October 1966
Place of birth: Dublin
Position: Centre-forward

Promotion campaign:
1998/99 league statistics: 36(3)18

A brilliant centre-forward and club legend, typically Niall Quinn was centre stage during the record-breaking promotion season of 1998/99. Niall was the fulcrum of the side, as he was throughout his time at the club. A superb target man who was top drawer at holding the ball up and bringing others into play, the Mighty Quinn also got on the scoresheet at a ratio of a goal per two starts. In total his tally reached 21 with the addition of three cup goals, including one in the League Cup semi-final at Leicester.

Eventual runners-up Bradford finished 18 points behind Sunderland but they were the second-best side in the division. Not only did Niall notch the only goal of the game when Sunderland went to Valley Parade, but when Thomas Sørensen got injured in that game Quinny went in goal and ensured a clean sheet.

Later, of course, he returned to take over the club, having pulled together the Drumaville Consortium. Niall managed Sunderland at the beginning of the 2006/07 promotion season before handing the reins over to Roy Keane, while he remained as chairman. Niall was inducted into the Sunderland Hall of Fame at the inaugural dinner in 2019.

———

RAE, Alex

Date of birth: 30 September 1969
Place of birth: Glasgow
Position: Midfield

Promotion campaign:
1998/99 league statistics: 12(3)2

Alex Rae was a rightfully popular player. An incisive passer with a combative edge to his game, he also had a goal in him. Unfortunately, problems in his personal life, combined with a series of injuries, meant that Alex didn't play anywhere near as much as his ability warranted in his time at the club. This was the case in the promotion season when his appearances came in two bursts of seven and eight consecutive games, the last of which came in mid-January. Both of his promotion season goals came in his first game of the campaign when he came off the bench to join in the goal fest as Oxford were beaten 7-0. Four years after his promotion with Sunderland Rae was a regular – alongside his fellow Sunderland promotion winner Paul Butler – as Wolves went up via the play-offs in which he scored in a semi-final win at Reading, but was an unused sub in the final.

_____

RIERA, Arnau
Date of birth: 1 October 1981
Place of birth: Manacor, Spain
Position: Midfield

Promotion campaign:
2006/07 league statistics: -(1)-

After over 150 games for Barcelona B where he had captained Lionel Messi, Arnau made an impressive debut as a sub in a dismal defeat at Southend. That performance earned him a start a few days later in a League Cup tie at Bury, but as chairman and manager Niall Quinn took his seat in the directors' box, he saw Arnau coming off after just three minutes. Having missed the opening minutes when making his way from the dressing room to his seat, Niall had to be told Arnau had just been sent off. He didn't play again!

_____

ROBINSON, Carl
Date of birth: 13 October 1976
Place of birth: Llandrindod Wells
Position: Midfield

Promotion campaign:
2004/05 league statistics: 40(-)4

Wales international Carl Robinson was a smooth operator. Mobile and tidy in possession, he was an excellent team player whose workmanlike approach did so much to help Sunderland control games. Like Keith Bertschin in the 1987/88 promotion season, 'Robbo' scored the first and last goals of the campaign. The latter was the only goal of the game on the day the Championship trophy was presented before a capacity crowd against Stoke, while one of his others provided a 1-0 win at Leeds.

Sunderland's promotion cost the club an additional £75,000 to Robinson's former employers Portsmouth, who he had left to sign for Sunderland in the summer of 2004 following a successful loan spell.

——

ROBSON, Bryan 'Pop'

Date of birth: 11 November 1945
Place of birth: Sunderland
Position: Forward

Promotion campaigns:
1975/76 league statistics: 40(-)13
1979/80 league statistics: 40(-)20

Pop Robson was top scorer in two promotion campaigns. A model professional who was a natural goalscorer, Robson had been the top flight's top scorer in his West Ham days in the season Sunderland won the FA Cup in 1972/73. His supreme balance owed a debt to his father-in-law Len Heppell, a professional ballroom dancer who went on to work with top stars across the sports world, from Bobby Moore to Frank Bruno to Björn Borg.

In total Robson had six spells with his home-town club, three of these as a player. He scored more goals in his opening season of 1974/75 than in 1975/76 when promotion was won but was still top scorer, three cup goals taking his tally to 16. His last goal of the season was the one that sealed promotion against Bolton Wanderers. Following a second spell with the Hammers, Robson returned to Roker Park in 1979 to fire Sunderland back into the top flight as top scorer once again.

——

ROSTRON, Wilf

Date of birth: 29 September 1956
Place of birth: Sunderland

Position: Midfield

Promotion campaign:
1979/80 league statistics: 8(-)-

An England schoolboys cap when at St Thomas Aquinas School in Sunderland, Wilf arrived at his home-town club in 1977 after starting with Arsenal. He returned to the south early in the promotion season, signing for Watford after starting eight of the first nine league games.

Rostron had also scored in the League Cup against Newcastle United in a first-leg game at Roker Park and added another in a penalty shoot-out to help win the tie. A versatile player who could play at full-back or on the wing as well as in midfield, he went on to play over 400 times for Watford, before spells with both Sheffield clubs prior to another return south with Brentford.

———

ROWELL, Gary

Date of birth: 6 June 1957
Place of birth: Seaham
Position: Midfield

Promotion campaigns:
1975/76 league statistics: 3(1)1
1979/80 league statistics: 8(9)-

Gary Rowell took over from Len Shackleton as Sunderland's record post-war scorer and remains one of only three players to have scored over a century of goals for the club since the war, Kevin Phillips having taken his record. What makes Rowell's goals tally particularly impressive is that he was primarily a midfielder, albeit his scoring record was boosted by being a brilliant penalty taker.

Rowell was the master of drifting into the box late and unnoticed. A great reader of the game, Gary had the knack of arriving in the right place at the right time to clinically convert chances.

A debutant during the 1975/76 Division Two-winning season, Rowell went on to be top scorer in five seasons out of six between 1977/78 and 1982/83. In the only season in that sequence where he wasn't top scorer Gary didn't score at all. That was the 1979/80 promotion campaign when he was coming back from a bad injury, but, nonetheless, he played his part in taking Sunderland up, not once but twice. Rowell was inducted into the club's Hall of Fame in 2020.

———

RUSSELL, Craig

Date of birth: 4 February 1974
Place of birth: Jarrow
Position: Forward

Promotion campaign:
1995/96 league statistics: 35(6)13

Top scorer as the championship trophy was won for the first time in the second tier (after the introduction of the Premiership), the Jarrow Arrow (or 'Jarra arra') was all about pace. A Sunderland supporter to the core, Craig had come through the youth team and was at his best when a ball was played in front of him to run on to. He would leave defenders trailing in his wake and had a cool head when it came to finishing. Manager Peter Reid often felt the need to utilise Russell on the right flank, but when he smashed four in a game against Millwall to take the Lads to the top of the table Russell's role was cemented as a central striker.

———

SCOTT, Martin

Date of birth: 7 January 1968
Place of birth: Sheffield
Position: Left-back

Promotion campaigns:
1995/96 league statistics: 43(-)6
1998/99 league statistics: 14(2)2

Scott was a first-class left-back who offered the added bonus of being an excellent penalty taker, as he won promotion at both Roker Park and the Stadium of Light. Four of his six goals in 1995/96 came from the spot as he was third-top scorer in a season where he missed just three games. That was Martin's best season at Sunderland. His second promotion season was his last at the club following a bad ankle injury sustained in an FA Cup third-round match at Lincoln. He had also been a Fourth Division title winner in 1989 with his first club Rotherham United.

———

SHARKEY, Nick
Date of birth: 4 May 1943
Place of birth: Helensburgh
Position: Forward

Promotion campaign:
1963/64 league statistics: 33 17

A nippy striker and the only man to score five goals in a game for Sunderland since World War Two, Sharkey came into the promotion side for the tenth league game of the season and from then on played every game. During the promotion season he added a further three goals in the FA Cup, including two against holders Manchester United. He also scored a hat-trick in a prestige friendly against Benfica, when he had another goal disallowed for someone else being offside. Sharkey also scored a hat-trick in the biggest win of the season against Swindon Town. A phenomenally prolific scorer at youth level, Nick first broke into the first team as a 16-year-old and overall averaged better than a goal every two games in his total of 117 games for the club.

———

SIDDALL, Barry
Date of birth: 12 September 1954
Place of birth: Ellesmere Port
Position: Goalkeeper

Promotion campaign:
1979/80 league statistics: 12(-)-

Barry Siddall had one of the toughest jobs in football in taking over from Jim Montgomery, but did it so well he became a cult hero in his own right. The keeper spawned numerous nicknames, being mainly – and affectionately – known as 'The Flying Pig', 'Seeedalll' and 'Basil', the latter due to being a lookalike of TV character Basil Fawlty.

There was nothing faulty about Siddall's goalkeeping. He was competent, brave and holds the record for the best penalty-saving record of any Sunderland goalie to face at least ten penalties, his 31 per cent success record being marginally better than that of Chris Turner, with whom he vied for the number one shirt during the promotion season.

Including games in the FA Cup, League Cup and Anglo-Scottish Cup, Siddall played 21 times during the campaign but only three of these came after early November. Although neither of his last two games of the term were lost, after conceding five goals Turner was instantly recalled and Siddall sat out the conclusion.

_____

SIMPSON, Danny

Date of birth: 4 January 1987
Place of birth: Salford
Position: Right-back

Promotion campaign:
2006/07 league statistics: 13(1)-

Simpson emulated fellow full-back Joe Hinnigan from the 1979/80 promotion season in playing 14 late-season games without being on the losing side; indeed, Simpson set a record for playing the most games without defeat in the entire career of any Sunderland player. He went on to win another Championship medal three years after his Sunderland one with Newcastle, another promotion in 2014 via the play-offs with QPR, and in 2016 became a Premier League winner with Leicester City.

SMITH, Martin

Date of birth: 13 November 1974
Place of birth: Sunderland
Position: Winger

Promotion campaigns:
1995/96 league statistics: 9(11)2
1998/99 league statistics: 4(4)3

A naturally talented footballer, Martin's promotion campaigns came in the third and sixth of his seasons at Sunderland, but after being a regular in his first two years in his final four campaigns, he started fewer league games in total than he had made in 1994/95. Being a regular substitute meant that he appeared in just under half the league games as the second tier was won in 1996.

In 1998/99 Martin found it even harder to get a game. Even after scoring twice in a 3-1 home win over Grimsby, Smith found himself back on the bench in the next league game. In between he had been one of the shoot-out scorers in a League Cup victory on penalties at Everton. Regularly used in the cups, Martin made just one fewer appearance in the cups than the league that term.

He went on to win a third promotion in 2005/06 with Northampton, who finished as runners-up to Carlisle in Coca-Cola Division Two (fourth tier).

SØRENSEN, Thomas

Date of birth: 12 June 1976
Place of birth: Frederica, Denmark
Position: Goalkeeper

Promotion campaign:
1998/99 league statistics: 45(-)-

Tasked by Peter Reid to find a new goalkeeper after Lionel Pérez's costly error late in the previous season's play-off final, Tony Coton recommended up-and-coming stopper Thomas Sørensen. The Dane went on to earn his place in the pantheon of great Sunderland goalkeepers, starting with the setting of a club record of clean sheets as promotion was won in his first season. Sørensen kept 24 clean sheets in his 45 games, his deputy Andy Marriott adding another in his only outing. Sørensen added a further five clean sheets in cup ties that season and by the time he left the club after five seasons had totalled 72 clean sheets, a tally only bettered in the entire history of the club by the legendary figures of Jim Montgomery, Ted Doig and Johnny Mapson.

_____

STEAD, Jon
Date of birth: 7 April 1983
Place of birth: Huddersfield
Position: Centre-forward

Promotion campaign:
2006/07 league statistics: 1(4)1

Jon Stead waited 1,706 minutes to score his first goal for Sunderland. It was the longest wait any SAFC striker had ever had before breaking his duck. That long-awaited first goal came from close range at Everton. His only other goal for Sunderland was a well-taken late strike in an otherwise dismal early-season promotion-year defeat at Southend, so home fans never got to see him score for the Lads.

Stead played in the first five games of the season under Niall Quinn as well as in the League Cup defeat to bottom of the entire Football League Bury. That was the night that chairman/manager Quinn announced a world-class figure was going to take over as manager. That man was Roy Keane who never selected Stead, who he swiftly loaned out to Derby before selling him to Sheffield United in the first available transfer window.

Jon won a promotion in 2020 when he came off the bench in the National League play-off final to assist Harrogate Town – for whom Sunderland's on-loan Jack Diamond was a scorer – to beat one of Stead's old clubs, Notts County, at Wembley.

STEWART, Marcus

Date of birth: 7 November 1972
Place of birth: Bristol
Position: Forward

Promotion campaign:
2004/05 league statistics: 40(3)16

Top scorer as promotion was won under Mick McCarthy, Stewart did well alongside Stephen 'Sleeves' Elliott, who scored one goal fewer than Marcus, with each of them adding a further cup goal to their tally. Stewart's promotion with Sunderland was one of three career promotions, as he also went up to the Premier League with Ipswich in 2000 and to League One with Exeter City in 2009. His triumph with Sunderland was the only time he was part of a league-winning side. In 2000/01 while with Ipswich he was the second-highest scorer in the Premier League, his 19 goals being bettered only by Jimmy Floyd Hasselbaink.

————

STEWART, Paul

Date of birth: 7 October 1964
Place of birth: Wythenshawe, Manchester
Position: Forward

Promotion campaign:
1995/96 league statistics: 11(1)1

An England international who won the FA Cup with Tottenham in 1991, Stewart came to Sunderland on loan from Liverpool in August 1995, but had the loan quickly terminated after being injured on his full debut. Six months later he returned on an initial short-term contract and made ten consecutive starts, scoring his only goal in the last of these as Birmingham City were beaten.

Three years after playing in a promotion season with Sunderland, as Sunderland were promoted again, so was the veteran Stewart, this time from the North-West Counties League to the Northern Premier League first division with Workington.

STOKES, Anthony

Date of birth: 25 July 1988
Place of birth: Dublin
Position: Forward

Promotion campaign:
2006/07 league statistics: 7(7)2

Backed by the Drumaville Consortium, Sunderland pushed the boat out financially to bring in this highly rated youngster from Arsenal in the January transfer window of 2007. Anthony never seemed to really fulfil his potential, though. His two goals in the campaign included one on the final day at Luton after promotion had already been sealed. He did win nine caps for the Republic of Ireland, seven pieces of silverware with Celtic and the Scottish Cup with Hibs. He also played in the Persian Gulf League, Greece and Turkey, but amidst a host of documented disciplinary problems was often best remembered for the tabloid headlines after he attacked an Elvis Presley impersonator!

SUMMERBEE, Nick

Date of birth: 28 August 1971
Place of birth: Altrincham
Position: Winger

Promotion campaign:
1998/99 league statistics: 36(-)3

Had the 'golden goal' been in operation in the 1998 play-off final, Summerbee would have scored it as he put Sunderland ahead in extra time at Wembley. The son of Manchester City and England great Mike, Summerbee went on to be a promotion hero the following season. In that great team of dynamic duos his partnership with right-back Chris Makin was superb. The pair understood each other's games as well as Superkev and Niall Quinn up front or 'Magic' Johnston and Mickey Gray on the opposite wing. The two flanks were totally different in style. While 'Magic' liked to beat his man and jink inside, Summerbee's style was to make half a yard and whip in delicious crosses so good that in his era only David Beckham could claim to be as good.

———

SWINBURNE, Trevor

Date of birth: 20 June 1953
Place of birth: East Rainton
Position: Goalkeeper

Promotion campaign:
1975/76 league statistics: 4(-)-

Coming from a family of goalkeepers, Trevor had the unenviable task of being reserve to the consistently brilliant Jim Montgomery. In total Swinburne managed just 13 appearances in a decade at Roker Park. During the Second Division championship season he played in the first two games and the last two after promotion was sealed. On the final day he kept a clean sheet against already-relegated Portsmouth as the championship was secured. His father Tom kept goal for Newcastle and was a wartime international, while brother Alan played briefly for Oldham.

———

THIRLWELL, Paul

Date of birth: 13 February 1979
Place of birth: Springwell, Washington
Position: Midfield

Promotion campaign:
1998/99 league statistics: 1(1)-

A debutant in an early-season League Cup win over York, four days later Paul made his league bow as a sub in a 5-0 win over Tranmere at the Stadium of Light. A couple of months later he got a full debut in another convincing win, 3-0 at Bolton, and otherwise was named on the bench four times in the league as well as playing in another couple of League Cup games. He went on to give the club good service and had an excellent career. In 2020, as assistant manager of

Harrogate Town, he helped the club into the Football League, where on-loan Sunderland youngster Jack Diamond scored in the Wembley play-off final for his side.

_____

THORNTON, Sean
Date of birth: 18 May 1983
Place of birth: Drogheda
Position: Midfield

Promotion campaign:
2004/05 league statistics: 3(13)4

That almost all of Thornton's appearances in his promotion season were as a sub is an illustration of the player not making the most of the talent he was blessed with. Naturally gifted, Sean was a creative playmaker and goalscorer who would have been eye-catching even if he hadn't decided to bleach his hair a very bright blonde. Manager Mick McCarthy went out of his way to try to get Sean to focus fully on his football and improve his lifestyle, but while Thornton was a nice lad, you always felt he needed that bit more professional discipline to make the most of the sort of talent that had no less a figure than Gianfranco Zola singing his praises after a Premier League meeting with Chelsea.

_____

TOWERS, Tony
Date of birth: 13 April 1952
Place of birth: Manchester
Position: Midfield

Promotion campaign:
1975/76 league statistics: 34(-)10

After captaining Sunderland to the Division Two title, Tony Towers won the only three full England caps of his career in the month after his club campaign came to an end. Towers oozed class in the centre of the park. His passing was crisp and penetrative, his tackling was well-timed and he carried a goal threat. A confident penalty taker, Tony reached double figures in goals as the league was won.

Earlier in his career he had both scored and been sent off against Sunderland during the 1973 cup run when he was with Manchester City and later came to Wearside as part of the deal that took cup winners Dennis Tueart and Mick Horswill to City, with whom he had won the European Cup Winners' Cup in 1970.

———

TRAIN, Ray

Date of birth: 10 February 1951
Place of birth: Nuneaton
Position: Midfield

Promotion campaign:
1975/76 league statistics: 12(-)-

Fewer than three weeks after scoring his second goal of the season for Carlisle against Sunderland, Ray Train was debuting for the Lads after Bob Stokoe paid £80,000 for him just before the old March transfer deadline.

Train was a 5ft 5in midfield dynamo who started every game to the end of the season from the time of his arrival. Train would play in every match up to Stokoe's autumn resignation, stay in the side under caretaker manager Ian MacFarlane, but quickly fall out of favour once Jimmy Adamson took over.

Twelve months after joining Sunderland, Train departed for under half what had been paid for him. Joining Bolton, he won a second Division Two title medal in three seasons when playing alongside Peter Reid in the Trotters' successful team of 1977/78 that also included Seamus McDonagh, Sam Allardyce and Frank Worthington, who would also have future spells on Wearside.

———

TURNER, Chris

Date of birth: 15 September 1958
Place of birth: Sheffield

Position: Goalkeeper

Promotion campaign:

1979/80 league statistics: 30(-)-

Signed at the start of the promotion season from Sheffield Wednesday by new manager Ken Knighton who knew him from their time at Hillsborough, Chris Turner was an outstanding goalkeeper.

Fairly small for a keeper at 5ft 10in, Turner was agile, brave and often inspirational. On many occasions he was the outstanding influence in games, notably in the run to the Milk (League) Cup Final in 1985, before he was sold for a joint club-record fee when he joined Manchester United as Sunderland lost the place in the top flight won in Turner's first season.

It didn't take Turner long to take over from Barry Siddall, after which Chris kept a dozen clean sheets in his 30 league appearances in the promotion campaign.

———

USHER, Brian

Date of birth: 11 March 1944

Place of birth: Broomside

Position: Winger

Promotion campaign:

1963/64 league statistics: 41 5

A debutant on the opening day of the first-ever promotion season, teenager Brian went on to miss just one game all year. A winger directed to get at his man and deliver early crosses, Usher provided much of the ammunition that was turned into goals. In addition to the first goal of the FA Cup run, Usher also scored the final goal of the league season. Promotion-winning manager Alan Brown later took him to Sheffield Wednesday where he was coached by Lawrie McMenemy, who he later played for at Doncaster where he still lives. Usher completed his days as a player with a spell at Yeovil in 1973, where he played for his 1964 promotion-winning team-mate Cec Irwin.

VARGA, Stanislav

Date of birth: 8 October 1972
Place of birth: Lipany, Slovakia
Position: Centre-back

Promotion campaign:
2006/07 league statistics: 20(-)1

Stan Varga will be forever famous at Sunderland for a phenomenal debut against Arsenal in 2000, only to be injured in his next game and never hit the same heights again. The giant Slovakian's promotion involvement came in his second spell at the club after he was signed by Roy Keane, who had played alongside him at Celtic where he had won league and cup medals. As Sunderland won promotion, Varga played regularly up to the turn of the year, but after Keane partnered Nyron Nosworthy in central defence with the on-loan newcomer Jonny Evans, Varga was restricted to a handful of times on the bench as an unused sub and an early February appearance in a home win over Coventry.

———

WAINWRIGHT, Neil

Date of birth: 4 November 1977
Place of birth: Warrington
Position: Winger

Promotion campaign:
1998/99 league statistics: -(2)-

Brought in from Wrexham for £100,000 at the start of the season, 'Wainy' was a back-up for top-class wingers who were in top form in Nicky Summerbee and Allan Johnston. He came off the bench in a couple of league games and made three cup appearances. As Sunderland went up to the Premier League, there would be no further league appearances for Neil, who managed three more cup games. He went on to play over 200 games for Darlington.

WALLACE, Ross

Date of birth: 23 May 1985
Place of birth: Dundee
Position: Winger

Promotion campaign:
2006/07 league statistics: 20(12)6

A lightning-fast winger, Wallace came from Celtic with Stan Varga as part of Roy Keane's transfer-deadline swoop for six players. Ross made an instant repayment in Keane's faith with a debut winner in the new manager's first game at Derby. It was the first of four winning goals Wallace scored as promotion was won, the other two earning a point and contributing to the big final day victory at Luton that clinched the Championship trophy.

Seven years after his promotion with Sunderland, Wallace was a promotion winner again with Burnley, while he made a clean sweep of the three major domestic Scottish honours during his stint with Celtic.

————

WARD, Darren

Date of birth: 11 May 1974
Place of birth: Worksop
Position: Goalkeeper

Promotion campaign:
2006/07 league statistics: 30(-)-

Ward was an excellent goalkeeper who was a model of calmness and consistency. Already competing for the first-team shirt with Hungary international Márton Fülöp, following promotion Ward had to cope with Craig Gordon coming in to take his place having commanded a British record fee for a goalkeeper. Ward himself was an international, winning five caps for Wales before his time with Sunderland.

WELSH, Andy

Date of birth: 24 November 1983
Place of birth: Manchester
Position: Winger

Promotion campaign:
2004/05 league statistics: 3(4)1

A wiry winger who appeared in seven league games in his promotion season and twice as many in the Premier League the following season. He was still at the club until three-quarters of the way through the following promotion season, although he spent much of the time out on loan to Leicester and didn't play for Sunderland at all that term, although he was an unused substitute back at Leicester.

―――

WHITEHEAD, Dean

Date of birth: 12 January 1982
Place of birth: Abingdon
Position: Midfield

Promotion campaigns:
2004/05 league statistics: 39(3)5
2006/07 league statistics: 43(2)4

Midfielder Whitehead was at his best when Sunderland didn't have the ball. That is not meant to be a derogatory description, quite the reverse. Not every player wants to put in the hard yards stopping the opposition from playing, closing down space and working hard to retrieve possession, but 'Deano' could never be faulted for his willingness to graft. When Sunderland did have the ball he did his best to keep it, his decision-making normally focussing on retaining possession.

Across two title-winning promotion seasons Dean played in all but five games and skippered the side to the 2006/07 championship. A decade later Whitehead featured in a third promotion to the Premiership when he played in 16 league games for Huddersfield Town, who went up on penalties in the play-off final, in which Dean was an unused sub.

WHITLEY, Jeff

Date of birth: 28 January 1979
Place of birth: Ndola, Zambia
Position: Midfield

Promotion campaign:
2004/05 league statistics: 32(3)-

Sunderland might not have needed to win promotion in 2004/05 but for Whitley's 'twinkle toes' penalty shoot-out failure in the previous season's play-off semi-final with Crystal Palace. The fact that Jeff stepped up to take a penalty, however, says everything about his character. A rare goalscorer and novice penalty taker, Whitley's function was to get around the pitch and graft, but he was always prepared to take responsibility. It was that attribute that encouraged Mick McCarthy to bring him to the club when the gaffer looked to transform the mentality following the grim relegation of 2003. Capped by Northern Ireland, Jeff had played in 42 games as Manchester City were promoted to the Premier League in 1999/2000.

―――

WHITWORTH, Steve

Date of birth: 20 March 1952
Place of birth: Ellistown, Leics
Position: Defender

Promotion campaign:
1979/80 league statistics: 42(-)-

Although he was the only ever-present in his promotion season, former England international right-back Whitworth remained distinctly underrated. No one could question his consistency, however, and he undoubtedly added quality to the side after joining in March 1979 following a decade with Leicester City.

A constructive player with the ball, Whitworth kept things simple and was all the more effective for that. While he would support the attack, careering forward on long-striding overlaps like the previous promotion-winning right-backs Cec Irwin and Dick Malone was not Steve's style. Using his experience, as captain Whitworth led by example. Having never scored in almost 400 league games at the time, the skipper stepped forward to score in a successful penalty shoot-out in the League Cup at Newcastle during the promotion season.

———

WILLIAMS, Darren

Date of birth: 28 April 1977
Place of birth: Middlesbrough
Position: Almost everywhere

Promotion campaigns:
1998/99 league statistics: 16(9)-
2004/05 league statistics: 1(-)-

During his nine seasons at Sunderland Darren Williams became renowned as the ultimate utility man. He was at his best in central defence, right-back or as a holding midfielder but would do a job wherever he was asked. Rarely would Darren be a match-winner but he was never a match-loser, as he was invariably dependable and resolute. He was also someone who always fully appreciated the backing of the fans and the role of the media. Nothing was ever too much trouble for him – undoubtedly one of the game's good guys.

The season before the 1998/99 promotion season had seen Darren mainly hold down a place in central defence, but with the arrival of Paul Butler, who was partnered with Andy Melville, 'Daz' was once again Peter Reid's go-to man when someone from the regular line-up was missing. There was also one appearance early in the 2004/05 promotion campaign, at Reading, in Williams's last term at the club.

———

WILLIAMS, Paul

Date of birth: 25 September 1970
Place of birth: Liverpool
Position: Full-back
Promotion campaign:
1989/90 league statistics: 1(-)- Play-offs -(-)-

Teenage full-back who, having debuted late the previous season, played in the 2-1 November win at Brighton and was also an unused sub for a home draw with Wolves a fortnight earlier. He was later left with restricted sight and went on to live in Colombia in South America, running a palm oil plantation.

———

WRIGHT, Stephen

Date of birth: 8 February 1980
Place of birth: Bootle
Position: Right-back

Promotion campaign:
2004/05 league statistics: 39(-)1
2006/07 league statistics: 2(1)-

Wright's first promotion season was the former Liverpool defender's best at Sunderland. He had played in 26 and 22 league games in his previous two seasons on Wearside but would appear in a total of only five league games across his next two seasons at the club. During 2004/05 Wright played in the vast majority of games and got on the scoresheet in an early-season home win over Nottingham Forest.

A tough, uncompromising full-back, Stephen was still at the club in 2006/07 but after playing in two of the first three games under Niall Quinn did not play again until the last day of the season when he was given a farewell appearance by Roy Keane. He had also been an unused sub at Barnsley in March on the day some players were left behind after being late for the coach.

———

YORKE, Dwight

Date of birth: 3 November 1971
Place of birth: Canaan, Tobago
Position: Midfield

Promotion campaign:
2006/07 league statistics: 28(4)5

Roy Keane rang his old Manchester United team-mate to persuade him to leave Sydney for Sunderland. The one-time top Old Trafford striker was winding down his playing days down under but was up for the challenge and didn't need convincing to swap the sights of the Opera House for the north-east.

At Sunderland, Dwight sat deep in midfield and orchestrated proceedings. His calmness in possession oozed class and confidence. This belief transmitted to the team as he fulfilled exactly the sort of role the gaffer wanted. He also found his old striking instincts intact when chances came his way, chipping in with five goals, four of them away from home.

APPENDIX

Results, appearances and final league tables.

Sunderland's score is always listed first in the table of results.
Home games are in bold.

1963/64 DIVISION TWO

Date	Opponent	R	Scorers	Attendance
Sat Aug 24	Huddersfield Town	2-0	Kerr, Mulhall	20,894
Wed Aug 28	**Portsmouth**	**3-0**	**Mulhall (2), Crossan**	**40,400**
Sat Aug 31	**Northampton Town**	**0-2**		**39,201**
Wed Sep 4	Portsmouth	4-2	Crossan (2), Kerr, Dickinson O.G.	16,520
Sat Sep 7	Bury	1-0	Usher	11,901
Mon Sep 9	Scunthorpe Utd.	1-1	Kerr	10,489
Sat Sep 14	**Manchester City**	**2-0**	**Crossan, Fogarty**	**39,298**
Wed Sep 18	**Scunthorpe Utd**	**1-0**	**Crossan**	**36,128**
Sat Sep 21	Swindon Town	0-1		26,273
Sat Sep 28	**Cardiff City**	**3-3**	**Sharkey (2), Hurley**	**37,287**
Wed Oct 2	Plymouth Argyle	1-1	Herd	13,609
Sat Oct 5	Norwich City	3-2	Hurley, McNab, Crossan	19,694
Wed Oct 9	**Newcastle Utd.**	**2-1**	**Ashurst, Herd**	**56,903**
Wed Oct 16	Derby County	3-0	Sharkey (2), Herd	20,305
Sat Oct 19	**Plymouth Argyle**	**1-0**	**Hurley**	**36,787**
Sat Oct 26	Middlesbrough	0-2		43,905
Sat Nov 2	**Grimsby Town**	**3-0**	**Crossan (2), Herd**	**29,004**
Sat Nov 9	Preston North End	1-1	Herd	26,579
Sat Nov 16	**Leyton Orient**	**4-1**	**Hurley, Mulhall, Crossan, Herd**	**35,004**
Sat Nov 23	Swansea Town	2-1	Hurley, Sharkey	10,880
Sat Nov 30	**Southampton**	**1-2**	**Crossan**	**34,998**

Sat Dec 7	Charlton Athletic	0-0		29,819
Sat Dec 14	**Huddersfield Town**	**3-2**	**Sharkey, Herd, Crossan (p)**	**27,417**
Sat Dec 21	Northampton Town	1-5	Herd	12,120
Thu Dec 26	Leeds Utd.	1-1	Mulhall	41,167
Sat Dec 28	**Leeds Utd.**	**2-0**	**Herd, Sharkey**	**55,046**
Sat Jan 11	**Bury**	**4-1**	**Crossan (2), Herd, Sharkey**	**36,962**
Sat Jan 18	Manchester City	3-0	Crossan (2, 1p), Mulhall	31,136
Sat Feb 1	**Swindon Town**	**6-0**	**Sharkey (3), Crossan (2) Usher**	**41,334**
Sat Feb 8	Cardiff City	2-0	Mulhall, Sharkey	15,600
Wed Feb 19	**Norwich City**	**0-0**		**44,514**
Sat Feb 22	**Derby County**	**3-0**	**Sharkey, Usher, Waller O.G.**	**43,945**
Sat Mar 7	**Middlesbrough**	**0-0**		**46,855**
Sat Mar 14	Newcastle United	0-1		27,341
Sat Mar 21	**Preston North End**	**4-0**	**Crossan, Mulhall, Sharkey (2)**	**35,420**
Fri Mar 27	**Rotherham Utd.**	**2-0**	**Herd (2)**	**56,675**
Mon Mar 30	Rotherham Utd.	2-2	Crossan (2)	21,641
Sat Apr 4	**Swansea Town**	**1-0**	**Usher**	**42,505**
Mon Apr 6	Leyton Orient	5-2	Bishop O.G., McNab, Crossan, Mulhall, Sharkey	16,133
Sat Apr 11	Southampton	0-0		21,944
Sat Apr 18	**Charlton Athletic**	**2-1**	**Herd, Crossan**	**50,827**
Sat Apr 25	Grimsby Town	2-2	Sharkey, Usher	16,442

Pos	Club	Pld	W	D	L	F	A	GA	Pts
1st	Leeds United	42	24	15	3	71	34	2.088	63
2nd	**Sunderland**	**42**	**25**	**11**	**6**	**81**	**37**	**2.189**	**61**
3rd	Preston North End	42	23	10	9	79	54	1.463	56
4th	Charlton Athletic	42	19	10	13	76	70	1.086	48
5th	Southampton	42	19	9	14	100	73	1.370	47
6th	Manchester City	42	18	10	14	84	66	1.273	45
7th	Rotherham United	42	19	7	16	90	78	1.154	45
8th	Newcastle United	42	20	5	17	74	69	1.072	45
9th	Portsmouth	42	16	11	15	79	70	1.129	43
10th	Middlesbrough	42	15	11	16	67	52	1.288	41
11th	Northampton Town	42	16	9	17	58	60	0.967	41
12th	Huddersfield Town	42	15	10	17	57	64	0.891	40
13th	Derby County	42	14	11	17	56	67	0.836	39
14th	Swindon Town	42	14	10	18	57	69	0.826	38
15th	Cardiff City	42	14	10	18	56	81	0.691	36
16th	Leyton Orient	42	13	10	19	54	72	0.750	36
17th	Norwich City	42	11	13	18	64	80	0.800	35

18th	Bury	42	13	9	20	57	73	0.781	35
19th	Swansea Town	42	12	9	21	63	74	0.851	33
20th	Plymouth Argyle	42	8	16	18	45	67	0.672	32
21st	Grimsby Town	42	9	14	19	47	75	0.627	32
22nd	Scunthorpe United	42	10	10	22	52	82	0.634	30

1975/76 DIVISION TWO

Date	Opponent	R	Scorers	Attendance
Sat Aug 16	**Chelsea**	**2-1**	**Robson, Longhorn**	**28,689**
Tue Aug 19	Bristol City	0-3		12,199
Sat Aug 23	Oxford United	1-1	Moncur	9,069
Tues Aug 26	**Fulham**	**2-0**	**Holden, Gibb**	**25,450**
Sat Aug 30	**Blackpool**	**2-0**	**Towers (2)**	**23,576**
Sat Sep 6	Plymouth Argyle	0-1		18,304
Sat Sep 13	**WBA**	**2-0**	**Halom, Hughes**	**25,159**
Sat Sep 20	Blackburn Rovers	1-0	Towers	15,773
Tue Sep 23	**Carlisle United**	**3-2**	**Robson, Towers (p), Hughes**	**28,185**
Sat Sep 27	**Notts County**	**4-0**	**Robson (2), Kerr, Halom**	**27,565**
Sat Oct 4	Portsmouth	0-0		13,577
Sat Oct 11	**Orient**	**3-1**	**Towers (p), Hughes, Robson**	**28,327**
Sat Oct 18	Bristol Rovers	0-1		13,577
Sat Oct 25	**Luton Town**	**2-0**	**Kerr, Robson**	**28,338**
Sat Nov 1	York City	4-1	Hughes, Hunter O.G., Towers (2, 1p)	15,232
Sat Nov 8	**Nottingham Forest**	**3-0**	**Robson, Halom (2)**	**31,227**
Sat Nov 15	Charlton Athletic	2-1	Holden (2)	22,307
Sat Nov 22	**Bristol Rovers**	**1-1**	**Kerr**	**31,356**
Sat Nov 29	**Oldham Athletic**	**2-0**	**Robson (2)**	**28,220**
Sat Dec 6	Southampton	0-4		17,598
Sat Dec 13	**Oxford United**	**1-0**	**Porterfield**	**22,501**
Sat Dec 20	Chelsea	0-1		22,802
Fri Dec 26	**Hull City**	**3-1**	**Holden, Finney, Henderson**	**35,210**
Sat Dec 27	Bolton Wanderers	1-2	Dunne O.G.	42,680
Sat Jan 10	WBA	0-0		25,399
Sat Jan 17	**Plymouth Argyle**	**2-1**	**Holden, Kerr**	**29,737**
Sat Feb 7	Fulham	0-2		2,839
Sat Feb 21	**Charlton Athletic**	**4-1**	**Holden, Moncur, Robson, Towers**	**30,173**
Tue Feb 24	Carlisle United	2-2	Towers (p), Holden	20,001
Sat Feb 28	Luton Town	0-2		15,338
Sat Mar 13	Orient	2-0	Kerr (2)	7,954
Wed Mar 17	Nottingham Forest	1-2	Holden	16,995
Sat Mar 20	Oldham Athletic	1-1	Hughes	13,704

Tues Mar 23	Bristol City	1-1	Holden		38,395
Sat Mar 27	Southampton	3-0	Greenwood (2), Holden		34,946
Tue Mar 30	York City	1-0	Kerr		33,462
Sat Apr 3	Notts County	0-0			14,811
Sat Apr 10	Blackburn Rovers	3-0	Holden, Parkes O.G., Robson		33,523
Sat Apr 17	Hull City	4-1	Robson, Rowell, Dobson O.G., Holden		21,296
Mon Apr 19	Bolton Wanderers	2-1	Towers (p), Robson		51,983
Tue Apr 20	Blackpool	0-1			16,768
Sat Apr 24	Portsmouth	2-0	Bolton, Hughes		40,515

Pos	Club	Pld	W	D	L	F	A	GA	Pts
1st	Sunderland	42	24	8	10	67	36	1.861	56
2nd	Bristol City	42	19	15	8	59	35	1.686	53
3rd	West Bromwich Albion	42	20	13	9	50	33	1.515	53
4th	Bolton Wanderers	42	20	12	10	64	38	1.684	52
5th	Notts County	42	19	11	12	60	41	1.463	49
6th	Southampton	42	21	7	14	66	50	1.320	49
7th	Luton Town	42	19	10	13	61	51	1.196	48
8th	Nottingham Forest	42	17	12	13	55	40	1.375	46
9th	Charlton Athletic	42	15	12	15	61	72	0.847	42
10th	Blackpool	42	14	14	14	40	49	0.816	42
11th	Chelsea	42	12	16	14	53	54	0.981	40
12th	Fulham	42	13	14	15	45	47	0.957	40
13th	Orient	42	13	14	15	37	39	0.949	40
14th	Hull City	42	14	11	17	45	49	0.918	39
15th	Blackburn Rovers	42	12	14	16	45	50	0.900	38
16th	Plymouth Argyle	42	13	12	17	48	54	0.889	38
17th	Oldham Athletic	42	13	12	17	57	68	0.838	38
18th	Bristol Rovers	42	11	16	15	38	50	0.760	38
19th	Carlisle United	42	12	13	17	45	59	0.763	37
20th	Oxford United	42	11	11	20	39	59	0.661	33
21st	York City	42	10	8	24	39	71	0.549	28
22nd	Portsmouth	42	9	7	26	32	61	0.525	25

1979/80 DIVISION TWO

Date	Opponent	R	Scorers	Attendance
Sat Aug 18	Chelsea	0-0		23,500
Wed Aug 22	Birmingham City	2-0	Robson, Brown	25,877
Sat Aug 25	Fulham	2-1	Arnott, Robson (p)	25,506
Sat Sep 1	Oldham Athletic	0-3		7,830
Sat Sep 8	Cambridge United	2-0	Buckley, Elliott	22,898

Sat Sep 15	West Ham United	0-2		24,021
Sat Sep 22	Burnley	1-1	Robson	8,751
Sat Sep 29	**Preston North End**	**1-1**	**Clarke**	**24,594**
Sat Oct 6	**Charlton Athletic**	**4-0**	**Hawley (3), Robson**	**24,865**
Tues Oct 9	Birmingham City	0-1		18,960
Sat Oct 13	Luton Town	0-2		13,504
Sat Oct 20	**QPR**	**3-0**	**Robson (2, 1p) Hawley**	**25,201**
Sat Oct 27	Leicester City	1-2	Lee	19,365
Sat Nov 3	**Chelsea**	**2-1**	**Arnott, Gilbert**	**24,968**
Sat Nov 10	Swansea City	1-3	Brown	15,826
Sat Nov 17	**Notts County**	**3-1**	**Robson (2, 1p), Cummins**	**21,896**
Sat Nov 24	**Bristol Rovers**	**3-2**	**Elliott, Cummins, Robson**	**21,292**
Sat Dec 1	Orient	1-2	Robson	6,582
Sat Dec 8	**Cardiff City**	**2-1**	**Davies O.G., Robson**	**25,370**
Sat Dec 15	Watford	1-1	Dunn	13,965
Fri Dec 21	**Shrewsbury Town**	**2-1**	**Marangoni, Arnott**	**21,237**
Wed Dec 26	**Wrexham**	**1-1**	**Arnott**	**29,567**
Sat Dec 29	Fulham	1-0	Marangoni	9,591
Tues Jan 1	Newcastle Utd	1-3	Cummins	38,322
Sat Jan 2	**Oldham Athletic**	**4-2**	**Brown (3), Robson**	**19,456**
Sat Jan 19	Cambridge Utd	3-3	Marangoni, Brown, Cummins	7,107
Sat Feb 9	**Burnley**	**5-0**	**Cummins (4), Arnott**	**21,855**
Sat Feb 16	Preston North End	1-2	Brown	12,165
Sat Feb 23	**Luton Town**	**1-0**	**Cooke**	**25,387**
Sat Mar 1	QPR	0-0		15,613
Sat Mar 8	**Leicester City**	**0-0**		**29,487**
Sat Mar 15	Charlton Athletic	4-0	Brown, Arnott, Robson (2)	6,185
Sat Mar 22	**Swansea City**	**1-1**	**Robson**	**25,175**
Sat Mar 29	Notts County	1-0	Cummins	10,878
Sat Apr 5	**Newcastle Utd**	**1-0**	**Cummins**	**41,752**
Mon Apr 7	Wrexham	1-0	Brown	12,064
Tues Apr 8	Shrewsbury Town	2-1	Robson, Cummins	12,345
Sat Apr 2	**Orient**	**1-1**	**Arnott**	**33,279**
Sat Apr 19	Bristol Rovers	2-2	Robson, Dunn	9,757
Sat Apr 26	**Watford**	**5-0**	**Robson (2), Buckley, Elliott (2)**	**32,195**
Sat May 3	Cardiff City	1-1	Robson	19,340
Mon May 12	**West Ham Utd**	**2-0**	**Arnott, Cummins**	**47,129**

Pos	Club	Pld	W	D	L	F	A	GA	Pts
1st	Leicester City	42	21	13	8	58	38	+20	55
2nd	**Sunderland**	**42**	**21**	**12**	**9**	**69**	**42**	**+27**	**54**

3rd	Birmingham City	42	21	11	10	58	38	+20	53
4th	Chelsea	42	23	7	12	66	52	+14	53
5th	Queens Park Rangers	42	18	13	11	75	53	+22	49
6th	Luton Town	42	16	17	9	66	45	+21	49
7th	West Ham United	42	20	7	15	54	43	+11	47
8th	Cambridge United	42	14	16	12	61	53	+8	44
9th	Newcastle United	42	15	14	13	53	49	+4	44
10th	Preston North End	42	12	19	11	56	52	+4	43
11th	Oldham Athletic	42	16	11	15	49	53	-4	43
12th	Swansea City	42	17	9	16	48	53	-5	43
13th	Shrewsbury Town	42	18	5	19	60	53	+7	41
14th	Orient	42	12	17	13	48	54	-6	41
15th	Cardiff City	42	16	8	18	41	48	-7	40
16th	Wrexham	42	16	6	20	40	49	-9	38
17th	Notts County	42	11	15	16	51	52	-1	37
18th	Watford	42	12	13	17	39	46	-7	37
19th	Bristol Rovers	42	11	13	18	50	64	-14	35
20th	Fulham	42	11	7	24	42	74	-32	29
21st	Burnley	42	6	15	21	39	73	-34	27
22nd	Charlton Athletic	42	6	10	26	39	78	-39	22

1987/88 DIVISION THREE

Date	Opponent	R	Scorers	Attendance
Sat Aug 15	Brentford	1-0	Bertschin	7,509
Sat Aug 22	**Bristol Rovers**	**1-1**	**Lemon**	**13,059**
Sat Aug 29	Doncaster Rovers	2-0	Lemon, Owers	2,740
Mon Aug 31	**Mansfield Town**	**4-1**	**Armstrong, Atkinson, MacPhail (2p)**	**13,994**
Sat Sept 5	Walsall	2-2	Bertschin (2)	6,909
Sat Sept 12	**Bury**	**1-1**	**Owers**	**13,227**
Tues Sept 15	Gillingham	0-0		9,184
Sat Sept 19	Brighton & HA	1-3	MacPhail (p)	8,949
Sat Sept 26	**Chester**	**0-2**		**12,760**
Tues Sept 29	Fulham	2-0	Gabbiadini (2)	6,996
Sat Oct 3	**Aldershot**	**3-1**	**MacPhail, Gabbiadini (2)**	**12,542**
Sat Oct 10	**Wigan Athletic**	**4-1**	**Gates (2) Gabbiadini (2)**	**13,974**
Sat Oct 17	Blackpool	2-0	MacPhail (2, 1p)	8,476
Tues Oct 20	Bristol City	1-0	Owers	15,109
Sat Oct 24	**York City**	**4-1**	**Cornforth (2), Gabbiadini, Gates**	**19,314**
Sat Oct 31	Notts County	1-2	MacPhail	8,854
Tues Nov 3	**Southend Utd**	**7-0**	**Gates (4), Atkinson (2), Gabbiadini**	**15,754**
Sat Nov 7	**Grimsby Town**	**1-1**	**Armstrong**	**18,197**

Sat Nov 21	Chesterfield	1-0	MacPhail (p)	5,700
Sat Nov 28	**Port Vale**	**2-1**	**Gates, MacPhail (p)**	**15,655**
Wed Dec 2	Northampton Town	2-0	Lemon, Gabbiadini	7,279
Sun Dec 20	**Rotherham Utd.**	**3-0**	**Gates (3)**	**20,168**
Sat Dec 26	Chester	2-1	MacPhail, Lemon	6,663
Mon Dec 28	**Preston NE**	**1-1**	**MacPhail (p)**	**24,818**
Fri Jan 1	**Doncaster Rovers**	**3-1**	**Gabbiadini, Leon (2)**	**19,419**
Sat Jan 2	Bury	3-2	Valentine O.G., Doyle, Gates	4,883
Sat Jan 16	**Brighton & HA**	**1-0**	**Lemon**	**17,404**
Sat Jan 30	**Gillingham**	**2-1**	**Bennett, Gabbiadini**	**16,195**
Sat Feb 6	**Walsall**	**1-1**	**Bennett**	**18,311**
Sat Feb 13	Preston NE	2-2	MacPhail, Gates	10,852
Sat Feb 20	**Brentford**	**2-0**	**Owers, Bertschin**	**15,458**
Wed Feb 24	Bristol Rovers	0-4		4,501
Sat Feb 27	Aldershot	2-3	MacPhail (p), Gabbiadini	5,010
Tues Mar 1	**Fulham**	**2-0**	**Armstrong, Gabbiadini**	**11,379**
Sat Mar 5	**Blackpool**	**2-2**	**Armstrong, Gates**	**15,513**
Sat Mar 12	Wigan Athletic	2-2	Gabbiadini, Gates	6,949
Sat Mar 19	**Notts County**	**1-1**	**Gabbiadini**	**24,071**
Sat Mar 26	York City	1-2	Pascoe	8,878
Sat Apr 2	Grimsby Town	1-0	Gabbiadini	7,001
Mon Apr 4	**Chesterfield**	**3-2**	**Lemon, Pascoe, Gabbiadini**	**21,886**
Sat Apr 9	Southend Utd	4-1	MacPhail (p), Lemon, Gabbiadini, Pascoe	8,109
Sat Apr 23	**Bristol City**	**0-1**		**18,225**
Tues Apr 26	Mansfield Town	4-0	Gates (2), Gabbiadini, Pascoe	6,930
Sat Apr 30	Port Vale	1-0	Gates	7,569
Mon May 2	**Northampton Town**	**3-1**	**MacPhail (p) Armstrong, Gates**	**29,454**
Sat May 7	Rotherham Utd	4-1	Gabbiadini (2), MacPhail (p), Bertschin	9,374

Pos	Club	Pld	W	D	L	F	A	GA	Pts
1st	**Sunderland**	**46**	**27**	**12**	**7**	**92**	**48**	**+44**	**93**
2nd	Brighton & Hove Albion	46	23	15	8	69	47	+22	84
3rd	Walsall	46	23	13	10	68	50	+18	82
4th	Notts County	46	23	12	11	82	49	+33	81
5th	Bristol City	46	21	12	13	77	62	+15	75
6th	Northampton Town	46	18	19	9	70	51	+19	73
7th	Wigan Athletic	46	20	12	14	70	61	+9	72
8th	Bristol Rovers	46	18	12	16	68	56	+12	66
9th	Fulham	46	19	9	18	69	60	+9	66
10th	Blackpool	46	17	14	15	71	62	+9	65
11th	Port Vale	46	18	11	17	58	56	+2	65

12th	Brentford	46	16	14	16	53	59	-6	62
13th	Gillingham	46	14	17	15	77	61	+16	59
14th	Bury	46	15	14	17	58	57	+1	59
15th	Chester City	46	14	16	16	51	62	-11	58
16th	Preston North End	46	15	13	18	48	59	-11	58
17th	Southend United	46	14	13	19	65	83	-18	55
18th	Chesterfield	46	15	10	21	41	70	-29	55
19th	Mansfield Town	46	14	12	20	48	59	-11	54
20th	Aldershot	46	15	8	23	64	74	-10	53
21st	Rotherham United	46	12	16	18	50	66	-16	52
22nd	Grimsby Town	46	12	14	20	48	58	-10	50
23rd	York City	46	8	9	29	48	91	-43	33
24th	Doncaster Rovers	46	8	9	29	40	84	-44	33

1989/90 DIVISION TWO

Date	Opponent	R	Scorers	Attendance
Sat Aug 19	Swindon Town	2-0	Gates, Hawke	10,199
Tues Aug 22	Ipswich Town	2-4	Gates, Gabbiadini	15,965
Sun Aug 27	Middlesbrough	2-1	Bennett, Pascoe	21,569
Sat Sept 2	WBA	1-1	Gabbiadini	10,885
Sat Sept 9	Watford	4-0	Armstrong, Gabbiadini (3)	15,042
Sat Sept 16	Blackburn Rovers	1-1	MacPhail	10,329
Sun Sept 24	Newcastle Utd	0-0		29,499
Wed Sept 27	Leicester City	3-2	Armstrong, Hardyman (p), Owers	10,843
Sat Sept 30	Sheffield Utd	1-1	Deane O.G.	22,760
Sat Oct 7	Bournemouth	3-2	Gates (2), Gabbiadini	15,933
Sat Oct 14	Leeds Utd.	0-2		27,815
Wed Oct 18	West Ham Utd	0-5		20,901
Sat Oct 21	Bradford City	1-0	MacPhail	14,849
Sat Oct 28	Stoke City	2-0	Bracewell, Gabbiadini	12,480
Tues Oct 31	Barnsley	4-2	Gates (2), Hardyman (p), Bennett	14,234
Sat Nov 4	Oldham Athletic	1-2	Owers	8,829
Sat Nov 11	Wolves	1-1	Hardyman (p)	20,660
Sat Nov 18	Plymouth Argyle	3-1	Gabbiadini, Owers, Ord	15,033
Sat Nov 25	Brighton & HA	2-1	Gabbiadini, Owers	8,681
Sat Dec 2	Swindon Town	2-2	Armstrong, Hauser	15,849
Sat Dec 9	Ipswich Town	1-1	Owers	13,833
Sat Dec 16	Portsmouth	3-3	Bennett, Hardyman, Gabbiadini	7,127
Tues Dec 26	Oxford Utd.	1-0	Gabbiadini	24,075
Sat Dec 30	Port Vale	2-2	Gabbiadini, Hauser	21,354
Mon Jan 1	Hull City	2-3	Hauser, Owers	9,346

Sun Jan 14	Middlesbrough	0-3	17,698		
Sat Jan 20	**WBA**	**1-1**	Gabbiadini		**15,583**
Sun Feb 4	Newcastle Utd.	1-1	Gabbiadini		31,572
Sat Feb 10	**Blackburn Rovers**	**0-1**			**16,043**
Sat Feb 17	Watford	1-1	Hauser		9,093
Sat Feb 24	**Brighton & HA**	**4-2**	Hauser (2)		**14,528**
Sat Mar 3	Plymouth Argyle	0-3			7,299
Sat Mar 10	**Leicester City**	**2-2**	Gabbiadini, Armstrong		**13,017**
Sat Mar 17	Bournemouth	1-0	Gabbiadini		6,328
Tues Mar 20	**Leeds Utd.**	**0-1**			**17,851**
Sat Mar 24	**West Ham Utd.**	**4-3**	Brady,Hardyman(p),Owers,Gabbiadini		13,896
Sat Mar 31	Bradford City	1-0	Brady		9,826
Tues Apr 3	Sheffield Utd.	3-1	Bracewell, Gabbiadini (2)		20,588
Sat Apr 7	**Stoke City**	**2-1**	Gabbiadini, Armstrong		**17,119**
Tues Apr 10	Barnsley	0-1			11,141
Sat Apr 14	**Hull City**	**0-1**			**17,437**
Mon Apr 16	Oxford Utd.	1-0	Gabbiadini		6,053
Sat Apr 21	**Portsmouth**	**2-2**	Armstrong (2)		**14,379**
Sat Apr 28	Wolves	1-0	Hardyman		19,463
Tues May 1	Port Vale	2-1	Owers, Hardyman		9,447
Sat May 5	**Oldham Athletic**	**2-3**	Owers, Armstrong		**22,243**

PLAY-OFFS

Sun May 13	**Newcastle Utd.**	**0-0**		**26,641**
Wed May 16	Newcastle Utd.	2-0	Gates, Gabbiadini	32,216
Mon May 28	Swindon Town	0-1		72,873

Pos	Club	Pld	W	D	L	F	A	GA	Pts
1st	Leeds United	46	24	13	9	79	52	+27	85
2nd	Sheffield United	46	24	13	9	78	58	+20	85
3rd	Newcastle United	46	22	14	10	80	55	+25	80
4th	Swindon Town	46	20	14	12	79	59	+20	74
5th	Blackburn Rovers	46	19	17	10	74	59	+15	74
6th	**Sunderland**	**46**	**20**	**14**	**12**	**70**	**64**	**+6**	**74**
7th	West Ham United	46	20	12	14	80	57	+23	72
8th	Oldham Athletic	46	19	14	13	70	57	+13	71
9th	Ipswich Town	46	19	12	15	67	66	+1	69
10th	Wolverhampton Wanderers	46	18	13	15	67	60	+7	67
11th	Port Vale	46	15	16	15	62	57	+5	61
12th	Portsmouth	46	15	16	15	62	65	-3	61
13th	Leicester City	46	15	14	17	67	79	-12	59

14th	Hull City	46	14	16	16	58	65	-7	58
15th	Watford	46	14	15	17	58	60	-2	57
16th	Plymouth Argyle	46	14	13	19	58	63	-5	55
17th	Oxford United	46	15	9	22	57	66	-9	54
18th	Brighton & Hove Albion	46	15	9	22	56	72	-16	54
19th	Barnsley	46	13	15	18	49	71	-22	54
20th	West Bromwich Albion	46	12	15	19	67	71	-4	51
21st	Middlesbrough	46	13	11	22	52	63	-11	50
22nd	AFC Bournemouth	46	12	12	22	57	76	-19	48
23rd	Bradford City	46	9	14	23	44	68	-24	41
24th	Stoke City	46	6	19	21	35	63	-28	37

1995/96 DIVISION ONE

Date	Opponent	R	Scorers	Attendance
Sat Aug 2	Leicester City	1-2	Agnew	18,593
Sat Aug 19	Norwich City	0-0		16,739
Sat Aug 26	Wolves	2-0	Melville, P. Gray	16,816
Wed Aug 30	Port Vale	1-1	P. Gray	7,693
Sat Sept 2	Ipswich Town	0-3		12,390
Sat Sept 9	Southend Utd.	1-0	Russell	13,805
Tues Sept 12	Portsmouth	1-1	Melville	12,282
Sat Sept 16	Luton Town	2-0	Mullin, P. Gray	6,955
Sat Sept 23	Millwall	2-1	Scott (p), Smith	8,691
Sat Sept 30	Reading	2-2	Kelly, Melville	17,503
Sat Oct 7	Crystal Palace	1-0	Kelly	13,754
Sat Oct 14	Watford	1-1	Scott	17,790
Sat Oct 21	Huddersfield Town	1-1	P. Gray	16,054
Sat Oct 28	Barnsley	2-1	Russell, Howey	17,024
Sun Nov 5	Charlton Athletic	1-1	M. Gray	11,626
Sat Nov 18	Sheffield Utd	2-0	P. Gray (2)	16,640
Wed Nov 22	Stoke City	0-1		11,754
Sat Nov 25	WBA	1-0	Howey	15,931
Sun Dec 3	Crystal Palace	1-0	Scott (p)	12,777
Sat Dec 9	Millwall	6-0	Scott(p), Russell (4), P. Gray	18,951
Sat Dec 16	Reading	1-1	Smith	9,431
Sat Dec 23	Derby County	1-3	M. Gray	16,882
Sun Jan 14	Norwich City	0-1		14,983
Sun Jan 21	Leicester City	0-0		16,130
Wed Jan 24	Grimsby Town	1-0	Ord	14,656
Tues Jan 30	Tranmere Rovers	0-0		17,616
Sat Feb 3	Wolves	0-3		26,537
Sat Feb 10	Port Vale	0-0		15,594

Sat Feb 17	Portsmouth	2-2	Agnew, Howey	12,241
Tues Feb 20	**Ipswich Town**	**1-0**	**Russell**	**14,052**
Sat Feb 24	**Luton Town**	**1-0**	**James O.G.**	**16,693**
Tues Feb 27	Southend Utd.	2-0	Scott (p), Bridges	5,786
Sun Mar 3	Grimsby Town	4-0	Ball, Russell, P. Gray, Bridges	5,318
Sat Mar 9	**Derby County**	**3-0**	**Russell (2), Agnew**	**21,644**
Tues Mar 2	Oldham Athletic	2-1	M. Gray, Ball	7,149
Sun Mar 17	Birmingham City	2-0	Agnew, Melville	23,251
Sat Mar 23	**Oldham Athletic**	**1-0**	**Scott**	**20,631**
Sat Mar 30	**Huddersfield Town**	**3-2**	**Ball, Bridges (2)**	**20,131**
Tues Apr 2	Watford	3-3	Agnew, Ball, Russell	11,195
Sat Apr 6	Barnsley	1-0	Russell	13,189
Mon Apr 8	**Charlton Athletic**	**0-0**		**20,914**
Sat Apr 13	Sheffield Utd.	0-0		20,050
Tues Apr 16	**Birmingham City**	**3-0**	**M. Gray, Stewart, Russell**	**19,831**
Sun Apr 21	**Stoke City**	**0-0**		**21,276**
Sat Apr 27	**WBA**	**0-0**		**22,027**
Sun May 5	Tranmere Rovers	0-2		16,193

Pos	Club	Pld	W	D	L	F	A	GA	Pts
1st	**Sunderland**	**46**	**22**	**17**	**7**	**59**	**33**	**+26**	**83**
2nd	Derby County	46	21	16	9	71	51	+20	79
3rd	Crystal Palace	46	20	15	11	67	48	+19	75
4th	Stoke City	46	20	13	13	60	49	+11	73
5th	Leicester City	46	19	14	13	66	60	+6	71
6th	Charlton Athletic	46	17	20	9	57	45	+12	71
7th	Ipswich Town	46	19	12	15	79	69	+10	69
8th	Huddersfield Town	46	17	12	17	61	58	+3	63
9th	Sheffield United	46	16	14	16	57	54	+3	62
10th	Barnsley	46	14	18	14	60	66	-6	60
11th	West Bromwich Albion	46	16	12	18	60	68	-8	60
12th	Port Vale	46	15	15	16	59	66	-7	60
13th	Tranmere Rovers	46	14	17	15	64	60	+4	59
14th	Southend United	46	15	14	17	52	61	-9	59
15th	Birmingham City	46	15	13	18	61	64	-3	58
16th	Norwich City	46	14	15	17	59	55	+4	57
17th	Grimsby Town	46	14	14	18	55	69	-14	56
18th	Oldham Athletic	46	14	14	18	54	50	+4	56
19th	Reading	46	13	17	16	54	63	-7	56
20th	Wolverhampton Wanderers	46	13	16	17	56	62	-8	55
21st	Portsmouth	46	13	13	20	61	69	-8	52

22nd	Millwall	46	13	13	20	43	63	-20	52
23rd	Watford	46	10	18	18	62	70	-8	48
24th	Luton Town	46	11	12	23	40	64	-45	45

1998/99 DIVISION ONE

Date	Opponent	R	Scorers	Attendance
Sat Aug 8	**QPR**	**1-0**	**Phillips (p)**	**40,537**
Sat Aug 15	Swindon Town	1-1	Phillips	10,207
Sat Aug 22	**Tranmere Rovers**	**5-0**	**Phillips, Dichio (2), Mullin, Butler**	**34,155**
Tues Aug 25	**Watford**	**4-1**	**Johnston, Summerbee, Dichio, Melville**	**36,587**
Sat Aug 29	Ipswich Town	2-0	Mullin, Phillips	15,818
Tues Sept 8	**Bristol City**	**1-1**	**Phillips**	**34,111**
Sat Sept 12	Wolves	1-1	Phillips	26,816
Sat Sept 19	**Oxford Utd.**	**7-0**	**Bridges (2), Gray, Dichio (2, 1p), Rae (2)**	**34,567**
Sat Sept 26	Portsmouth	1-1	Johnston	17,022
Tues Sept 29	Norwich City	2-2	Quinn, Marshall A. O.G.	17,504
Sat Oct 3	**Bradford City**	**0-0**		**37,828**
Sun Oct 18	WBA	3-2	Melville, Bridges, Ball	14,746
Wed Oct 21	Huddersfield Town	1-1	Ball	20,741
Sat Oct 24	**Bury**	**1-0**	**Dichio**	**38,049**
Sun Nov 1	Bolton Wanderers	3-0	Johnston, Quinn, Bridges	21,676
Tues Nov 3	Crewe Alexandra	4-1	Dichio, Gray, Quinn, Bridges	5,361
Sat Nov 7	**Grimsby Town**	**3-1**	**Smith (2), Quinn**	**40,077**
Sat Nov 14	Port Vale	2-0	Aspin O.G., Quinn	8,839
Sat Nov 21	**Barnsley**	**2-3**	**Scott (p), Quinn**	**40,231**
Sat Nov 28	Sheffield Utd.	4-0	Quinn (2), Bridges (2)	25,612
Sat Dec 5	**Stockport County**	**1-0**	**Summerbee**	**36,040**
Sat Dec 12	**Port Vale**	**2-0**	**Smith, Butler**	**37,583**
Tues Dec 15	**Crystal Palace**	**2-0**	**Scott (p), Dichio**	**33,870**
Sat Dec 19	Birmingham City	0-0		22,095
Sat Dec 26	Tranmere Rovers	0-1		14,248
Mon Dec 28	**Crewe Alexandra**	**2-0**	**Dichio, Bridges**	**41,433**
Sat Jan 9	QPR	2-2	Phillips, Quinn	17,444
Sun Jan 17	**Ipswich Town**	**2-1**	**Quinn (2)**	**39,835**
Sat Jan 30	Watford	1-2	Quinn	20,188
Sat Feb 6	**Swindon Town**	**2-0**	**Quinn, Phillips**	**41,304**
Sat Feb 13	Bristol City	1-0	Phillips (p)	15,736
Sat Feb 20	**Wolves**	**2-1**	**Johnston, Quinn**	**41,268**
Sat Feb 27	Oxford Utd	0-0		9,044
Tues Mar 2	**Portsmouth**	**2-0**	**Dichio, Phillips**	**37,656**
Sat Mar 6	**Norwich City**	**1-0**	**Phillips**	**39,004**
Tues Mar 9	Bradford City	1-0	Quinn	15,124

Sat Mar 13	Grimsby Town	2-0	Phillips, Clark		9,528
Sat Mar 20	**Bolton Wanderers**	**3-1**	**Phillips, Johnston (2)**		**41,505**
Sat Apr 3	**WBA**	**3-0**	**Phillips (2), Clark**		**41,135**
Mon Apr 5	Crystal Palace	1-1	Phillips		22,096
Sat Apr 10	**Huddersfield Town**	**2-0**	**Quinn, Johnston**		**41,074**
Tues Apr 13	Bury	5-2	Phillips (4, 1p), Quinn		8,669
Fri Apr 16	Barnsley	3-1	Summerbee, Clark, Phillips		17,390
Sat Apr 24	**Sheffield Utd.**	**0-0**			**41,179**
Sat May 1	Stockport County	1-1	Phillips		10,548
Sun May 9	**Birmingham City**	**2-1**	**Phillips, Quinn**		**41,634**

Pos	Club	Pld	W	D	L	F	A	GA	Pts
1st	**Sunderland**	**46**	**31**	**12**	**3**	**91**	**28**	**+63**	**105**
2nd	Bradford City	46	26	9	11	82	47	+35	87
3rd	Ipswich Town	46	26	8	12	69	32	+37	86
4th	Birmingham City	46	23	12	11	66	37	+29	81
5th	Watford	46	21	14	11	65	56	+9	77
6th	Bolton Wanderers	46	20	16	10	78	59	+19	76
7th	Wolverhampton Wanderers	46	19	16	11	64	43	+21	73
8th	Sheffield United	46	18	13	15	71	66	+5	67
9th	Norwich City	46	15	17	14	62	61	+1	62
10th	Huddersfield Town	46	15	16	15	62	71	-9	61
11th	Grimsby Town	46	17	10	19	40	52	-12	61
12th	West Bromwich Albion	46	16	11	19	69	76	-7	59
13th	Barnsley	46	14	17	15	59	56	+3	59
14th	Crystal Palace	46	14	16	16	58	71	-13	58
15th	Tranmere Rovers	46	12	20	14	63	61	+2	56
16th	Stockport County	46	12	17	17	49	60	-11	53
17th	Swindon Town	46	13	11	22	59	81	-22	50
18th	Crewe Alexandra	46	12	12	22	54	78	-24	48
19th	Portsmouth	46	11	14	21	57	73	-16	47
20th	Queens Park Rangers	46	12	11	23	52	61	-9	47
21st	Port Vale	46	13	8	25	45	75	-30	47
22nd	Bury	46	10	17	19	35	60	-25	47
23rd	Oxford United	46	10	14	22	48	71	-23	44
24th	Bristol City	46	9	15	22	57	80	-23	42

2004/05 CHAMPIONSHIP

Date	Opponent	R	Scorers	Attendance
Sat Aug 7	Coventry City	0-2		16,460
Tues Aug 10	**Crewe Alexandra**	**3-1**	**Robinson, Stewart, Elliott**	**22,341**

Sat Aug 14	**QPR**	**2-2**	**Stewart, Caldwell**	**26,063**
Sat Aug 21	Plymouth Argyle	1-2	Stewart	16,874
Sat Aug 28	**Wigan Athletic**	**1-1**	**Elliott**	**26,330**
Tues Aug 31	Reading	0-1		15,792
Sat Sept 11	Gillingham	4-0	Stewart (3), Elliott	8,775
Tues Sept 14	**Nottingham Forest**	**2-0**	**Arca, Wright**	**23,450**
Sat Sept 18	**Preston NE**	**3-1**	**Elliott (2), Carter**	**24,264**
Fri Sept 24	Leeds Utd.	1-0	Robinson	28,926
Tues Sept 28	Sheffield Utd.	0-1		17,908
Sat Oct 2	**Derby County**	**0-0**		**29,881**
Sat Oct 16	**Millwall**	**1-0**	**Muscat O.G.**	**23,839**
Tues Oct 19	Watford	1-1	Elliott	13,198
Mon Oct 25	Rotherham Utd.	1-0	Whitehead	6,026
Sat Oct 30	**Brighton & HA**	**2-0**	**Arca, Lawrence (p)**	**25,532**
Tues Nov 2	**Wolves**	**3-1**	**Lawrence (2), Elliott**	**23,925**
Fri Nov 5	Millwall	0-2		10,513
Sat Nov 13	Leicester City	1-0	Caldwell	25,817
Sun Nov 21	**Ipswich Town**	**2-0**	**Elliott, Brown**	**31,723**
Sat Nov 27	Stoke City	1-0	Bridges	16,980
Sat Dec 4	**West Ham Utd.**	**0-2**		**29,510**
Sat Dec 11	Cardiff City	2-0	Whitehead, Lawrence	12,528
Sat Dec 18	**Burnley**	**2-1**	**Arca, Bridges**	**27,102**
Sun Dec 26	**Leeds Utd.**	**2-3**	**Lawrence (p), Arca**	**43,253**
Tues Dec 8	Nottingham Forest	2-1	Elliott, Stewart	27,457
Sat Jan 1	Preston NE	2-3	Elliott, Thornton	16,940
Mon Jan 3	**Gillingham**	**1-1**	**Brown**	**27,147**
Sun Jan 16	Derby County	2-0	Elliott, Whitehead	22,995
Sat Jan 22	**Sheffield Utd.**	**1-0**	**Stewart**	**27,337**
Fri Feb 4	Wolves	1-1	Elliott	26,968
Sat Feb 12	**Watford**	**4-2**	**Stewart (3, 1p), Brown**	**24,948**
Sat Feb 19	Brighton & HA	1-2	Arca	6,647
Tues Feb 22	**Rotherham Utd.**	**4-1**	**Whitehead, Thornton (2), Breen**	**22,267**
Sat Feb 26	**Cardiff City**	**2-1**	**Breen, Stewart**	**32,778**
Fri Mar 4	Burnley	2-0	Lawrence, Stewart	12,103
Sat Mar 12	Crewe Alexandra	1-0	Elliott	7,949
Tues Mar 15	**Plymouth Argyle**	**5-1**	**Whitehead, Arca, Stewart(p), Caldwell, Thornton**	**25,258**
Sat Mar 19	**Coventry City**	**1-0**	**Brown**	**29,424**
Sat Apr 2	QPR	3-1	Welsh, Brown, Arca	18,198
Tues Apr 5	Wigan Athletic	1-0	Stewart	20,745
Sat Apr 9	**Reading**	**1-2**	**Arca**	**34,237**

Sun Apr 17	Ipswich Town	2-2	Elliott, Robinson		29,230
Sat Apr 23	**Leicester City**	**2-1**	**Stewart, Caldwell**		**34,815**
Fri Apr 29	West Ham Utd	2-1	Arca, Elliott		33,482
Sun May 8	**Stoke City**	**1-0**	**Robinson**		**47,350**

Pos	Club	Pld	W	D	L	F	A	GA	Pts
1st	**Sunderland**	**46**	**29**	**7**	**10**	**76**	**41**	**+35**	**94**
2nd	Wigan Athletic	46	25	12	9	79	35	+44	87
3rd	Ipswich Town	46	24	13	9	85	56	+29	85
4th	Derby County	46	22	10	14	71	60	+11	76
5th	Preston North End	46	21	12	13	67	58	+9	75
6th	West Ham United	46	21	10	15	66	56	+10	73
7th	Reading	46	19	13	14	51	44	+7	70
8th	Sheffield United	46	18	13	15	57	56	+1	67
9th	Wolverhampton Wanderers	46	15	21	10	72	59	+13	66
10th	Millwall	46	18	12	16	51	45	+6	66
11th	Queens Park Rangers	46	17	11	18	54	58	-4	62
12th	Stoke City	46	17	10	19	36	38	-2	61
13th	Burnley	46	15	15	16	38	39	-1	60
14th	Leeds United	46	14	18	14	49	52	-3	60
15th	Leicester City	46	12	21	13	49	46	+3	57
16th	Cardiff City	46	13	15	18	48	51	-3	54
17th	Plymouth Argyle	46	14	11	21	52	64	-12	53
18th	Watford	46	12	16	18	52	59	-7	52
19th	Coventry City	46	13	13	20	61	73	-12	52
20th	Brighton & Hove Albion	46	13	12	21	40	65	-25	51
21st	Crewe Alexandra	46	12	14	20	66	86	-20	50
22nd	Gillingham	46	12	14	20	45	66	-21	50
23rd	Nottingham Forest	46	9	17	20	42	66	-24	44
24th	Rotherham United	46	5	14	27	35	69	-34	29

2006/07 CHAMPIONSHIP

Date	Opponent	R	Scorers	Attendance
Sun Aug 6	Coventry City	1-2	Murphy	22,366
Wed Aug 9	**Birmingham City**	**0-1**		**26,668**
Sat Aug 12	**Plymouth Argyle**	**2-3**	**Murphy, S. Elliott**	**24,377**
Sat Aug 19	Southend Utd.	1-3	Stead	9,848
Mon Aug 28 WBA		**2-0**	**Whitehead, N. Collins**	**24,242**
Sat Sept 9	Derby County	2-1	Brown, Wallace	26,502
Wed Sept 13	Leeds Utd.	3-0	L. Miller, Kavanagh, S. Elliott	23,037

Sat Sept 16	**Leicester City**	**1-1**	**Hysen**	**35,104**
Sat Sept 23	Ipswich Town	1-3	De Vos O.G.	23,311
Sat Sept 30	**Sheffield Wednesday**	**1-0**	**Leadbitter**	**36,764**
Sat Oct 14	Preston NE	1-4	Varga	19,603
Tues Oct 17	Stoke City	1-2	Yorke	14,482
Sat Oct 21	**Barnsley**	**2-0**	**Whitehead, Brown**	**27,918**
Sat Oct 28	Hull City	1-0	Wallace	21,512
Tues Oct 31	**Cardiff City**	**1-2**	**Brown**	**26,528**
Sat Nov 4	Norwich City	0-1		24,652
Sat Nov 11	**Southampton**	**1-1**	**Wallace**	**25,667**
Sat Nov 18	**Colchester Utd.**	**3-1**	**S. Elliott (2), Connolly**	**25,197**
Fri Nov 24	Wolves	1-1	S. Elliott	27,203
Tues Nov 28	QPR	2-1	Murphy, Leadbitter	13,108
Sat Dec 2	**Norwich City**	**1-0**	**Murphy**	**27,934**
Sat Dec 9	**Luton Town**	**2-1**	**Murphy, Connolly**	**30,445**
Sat Dec 16	Burnley	2-2	Leadbitter, Connolly	14,798
Fri Dec 22	Crystal Palace	0-1		17,439
Tues Dec 26	**Leeds Utd.**	**2-0**	**Connolly, Leadbitter**	**40,116**
Sat Dec 30	**Preston NE**	**0-1**		**30,460**
Mon Jan 1	Leicester City	2-0	Hysen, Connolly	21,975
Sat Jan 13	**Ipswich Town**	**1-0**	**Connolly**	**27,604**
Sat Jan 20	Sheffield Wednesday	4-2	Yorke, Hysen, Connolly, Edwards	29,103
Tues Jan 30	**Crystal Palace**	**0-0**		**26,958**
Sat Feb 3	**Coventry City**	**2-0**	**Yorke, Edwards**	**33,591**
Sat Feb 10	Plymouth Argyle	2-0	Stokes, Connolly	15,247
Sat Feb 17	**Southend Utd.**	**4-0**	**Connolly, Hysen, John (2)**	**33,576**
Tues Feb 20	Birmingham City	1-1	Edwards	20,941
Sat Feb 24	**Derby County**	**2-1**	**Connolly (p), Miller**	**36,049**
Sat Mar 3	WBA	2-1	Yorke, John	23,252
Sat Mar 10	Barnsley	2-0	Leadbitter, Connolly	18,207
Tues Mar 13	**Stoke City**	**2-2**	**Whitehead, Murphy**	**31,358**
Sat Mar 17	**Hull City**	**2-0**	**Evans, John**	**38,448**
Sat Mar 31	Cardiff City	1-0	Wallace	19,353
Sat Apr 7	**Wolves**	**2-1**	**Murphy, Wallace**	**40,748**
Mon Apr 9	Southampton	2-1	Edwards, Leadbitter	25,766
Sat Apr 14	**QPR**	**2-1**	**Whitehead, Leadbitter**	**39,206**
Sat Apr 21	Colchester Utd.	1-3	Yorke	6,042
Fri Apr 27	**Burnley**	**3-2**	**Murphy, Connolly (p), Edwards**	**44,448**
Sun May 6	Luton Town	5-0	Stokes, Murphy (2), Wallace, Connolly	10,260

Pos	Club	Pld	W	D	L	F	A	GA	Pts
1st	**Sunderland**	**46**	**27**	**7**	**12**	**76**	**47**	**+29**	**88**
2nd	Birmingham City	46	26	8	12	67	42	+25	86
3rd	Derby County	46	25	9	12	62	46	+16	84
4th	West Bromwich Albion	46	22	10	14	81	55	+26	76
5th	Wolverhampton Wanderers	46	22	10	14	59	56	+3	76
6th	Southampton	46	21	12	13	77	53	+24	75
7th	Preston North End	46	22	8	16	64	53	+11	74
8th	Stoke City	46	19	16	11	62	41	+21	73
9th	Sheffield Wednesday	46	20	11	15	70	66	+4	71
10th	Colchester United	46	20	9	17	70	56	+14	69
11th	Plymouth Argyle	46	17	16	13	63	62	+1	67
12th	Crystal Palace	46	18	11	17	59	51	+8	65
13th	Cardiff City	46	17	13	16	57	53	+4	64
14th	Ipswich Town	46	18	8	20	64	59	+5	57
15th	Burnley	46	15	12	19	52	49	+3	57
16th	Norwich City	46	16	9	21	56	71	-15	57
17th	Coventry City	46	16	8	22	47	62	-15	56
18th	Queens Park Rangers	46	14	11	21	54	68	-14	53
19th	Leicester City	46	13	14	19	49	64	-15	53
20th	Barnsley	46	15	5	26	53	85	-32	50
21st	Hull City	46	13	10	23	51	67	-16	49
22nd	Southend United	46	10	12	24	47	80	-33	42
23rd	Luton Town	46	10	10	26	53	81	-28	40
24th	Leeds United	46	13	7	26	46	72	-26	36*